Appraising Moving Images

Appraising Moving Images

Assessing the Archival and Monetary Value of Film and Video Records

Sam Kula

The Scarecrow Press, Inc.
Lanham, Maryland, and Oxford
2003

SCARECROW PRESS, INC.

Published in the United States of America
by Scarecrow Press, Inc.
A Member of the Rowman & Littlefield Publishing Group
4720 Boston Way, Lanham, Maryland 20706
www.scarecrowpress.com

PO Box 317
Oxford
OX2 9RU, UK

Copyright © 2002 by Sam Kula

British Library Cataloguing in Publication Information Available

Library of Congress Control Number: 2002110539

ISBN 0-8108-4368-4 (cloth : alk. paper)

Printed in the United States of America

♾™ The paper used in this publication meets the minimum requirements of American
National Standard for Information Sciences—Permanence of Paper for Printed Library
Materials, ANSI/NISO Z39.48–1992.

for Bunty

for the dissertation that got away

Contents

Introduction

In archives, the only thing that really matters is the quality of the collections; all the rest is housekeeping. *

By the end of the twentieth century the sheer volume of contemporary records in all formats threatened to inundate the custodial institutions (archives, libraries, museums) of the world. Appraisal and selection were no longer options but essential elements in the archival process. The so-called paperless office that was supposed to have arrived with electronic communication in the Digital Age has had very little impact in diminishing the volume. Printers all over the world are working overtime creating permanent records from e-mail and computer files. The exponential increase in electronic communication has raised serious issues with regard to authenticity and the evidential value of the record (even what exactly constitutes a record in networked communications is at issue) at the same time as it presented the archivist with a host of new problems in long-term preservation.

Despite the inarguable theoretical objections to selection advanced by Jenkinson and others (neither the historian nor the archivist [or ultimate custodian] should share in the creation of archives), the dual pressures of space and cost, and critical factors in controlling digital records in pre- and post-custodial modes, are forcing all archivists to adopt at least some of the proposals advanced by Schellenberg for modern archives management, proposals in which appraisal and selection are deeply embedded.[1] Not only has appraisal become a leading issue in the archival literature, with strategies such as macro-appraisal and documentation strategy, appraisal methodology is being applied earlier and earlier in the life cycle to the point where record creation itself is being managed.

Appraisal remains, however, the most sensitive aspect of archives administration, what Gerald Ham called "our most important and intellectually demanding task as archivists."[2] Appraisal leaves the custodian open to allegations of subjectivity or prejudice, regarding records selected, or charges of incompetence, if not criminal negligence, regarding records destroyed. Decisions are made, nevertheless, even though the policies on which they are based are seldom precise or unequivocal. And even if the policies were clear and consistent, it is doubtful whether they would be interpreted in the same way in another organization, in another country, or by the next generation of archivists.

The uneasiness with which custodians now approach the appraisal and selection of traditional paper records—the record groups, series, and files that represent the administrative history of a government department or a private organization, as well as constituting a record of its activities—is intensified when the archivist is faced with nontextual records. If little exists in the way of guidelines or uniform practice when dealing with traditional paper records, there is even less when the newer media are at issue. Since moving image records are seldom part of records series, and therefore firmly grounded as to provenance and evidentiary function, they are not readily assessable in the context of the activity that initiated their production. Moving images produced outside of direct governmental sponsorship—the so-called private sector (frequently operating with government subsidies if not under government direction) in countries where film and television production are not state monopolies—are even more difficult to appraise using the selection criteria developed for government records.

Henri Langlois, the legendary founder of the Cinémathèque Françaises in Paris and one of the founders of the International Federation of Film Archives, always maintained that any selection policy was indefensible, that no archivist had the right to play God in determining which films would live and which would die.[3] The position is theoretically unassailable, and when only a relative handful of titles were accessible for archival conservation in the chaos of the immediate postwar years in Europe, the policy of total inclusion was probably the only practical one to adopt. As the volume of production increased, however, and the moving image archives, operating without a copyright or mandatory deposit law, had to actively solicit acquisitions through voluntary deposit, choices were made of necessity. The film archivist, by acting to save only certain titles, was inevitably condemning other titles to the vicissitudes of the marketplace. In the absence of an articulated appraisal and selection policy the accessions that were made took on the character of accident, or administrative convenience, or allegiance to fashion in selecting the critical and/or popular successes of the day.

That there were only a handful of institutions throughout the world actively acquiring and conserving motion pictures in the first fifty years following the invention of cinematography, and that those were exclusively nongovernmental museums and cinematheques, perhaps explains the scarcity of references to the archival preservation of moving images in the literature of the day. Appraisal and selection policy had to wait for a more serious engagement with moving images by a broad spectrum of custodial institutions. This has now occurred in many countries and the pervasive influence of television is accelerating the process. In many countries without a history of motion picture production, the archival preservation of moving images is a direct outgrowth of the advent of television broadcasting, and the concern that this aspect of the cultural heritage, linked as it is with many other aspects of the culture, should not be lost

Although the International Federation of Film Archives was originally established in 1938, it was not until 1972 that the International Council on Archives (ICA) took official recognition of moving images in a report entitled Archives of Motion Pictures, Photographic Records and Sound Recordings prepared by Wilhelm Kohte for the Moscow Congress. Following a report on the archives of film, television, and radio, which I prepared for the London Congress in 1980, the ICA established a Working Group on Audio-Visual Records, which I chaired through its formative years. At about the same time the Society of American Archivists set up a committee on audiovisual records which was linked through common membership with the Film Archives Advisory Committee/Television Archives Advisory Committee, a coordinating body established by my office, as Archivist of the American Film Institute, 1968-1973, on behalf of the National Endowment of the Arts in Washington, D.C.

UNESCO's link with the movement until 1980 was through the International Film and Television Council and its efforts (without, alas, much success) to establish international standards for the cataloging of moving images at least for the purposes of international exchanges. In the past twenty years there has been a vast increase in the number of custodial institutions, both governmental as well as nongovernmental, that have accepted responsibility for moving images in an era when the volume of production makes appraisal and selection not an option, but a critical necessity.

Appraising moving images remains a necessity despite the claims made for digitization and the possibilities of compression to reduce the

vast quantities of tape or discs that digitization now requires. None of
the digital storage media that have been introduced to date are "archival," either in terms of longevity of the medium or the survival of the
equipment necessary to access the recordings. All they have succeeded
in doing is vastly complicating the life of the moving image archivist!

Part of the growth in the number of moving image archives over
the past twenty years may be linked to *Recommendation for the Safeguarding and Preservation of Moving Images*, adopted by the General
Assembly of UNESCO at the 1980 Belgrade Conference. The objective
of the *Recommendation* is that all moving image documents of cultural,
historical, or social significance be deposited and conserved in official
archives, designated or established for the purpose.

The archival appraisal of moving images is still a relatively new
concept, and one that is not universally accepted as necessary or wise.
Several of my colleagues in the field stand firm with Langlois in the
belief that it is dangerous, or at the very least an inherently damaging
practice to be avoided at all costs. Many hold to the belief that compulsory deposit of every audiovisual work in a designated public institution, as books are deposited in national libraries, will make selection
unnecessary. It may not be possible for any one institution to do this,
but a network of institutions working in cooperation could preserve
every production.

This belief is usually associated with the expectation that new
technology will somehow diminish the vast storage capacity and limit
the vast processing funding that will be necessary if every production is
preserved, and eliminate the need to migrate the recordings to new media for public access or long-term preservation. As I write this there is a
spirited discussion taking place on the Association of Moving Image
Archivist's list-serve (amia-l@lsv.uky.edu) on the viability of using
vast capacity servers, disc drives linked together, as *virtual archives* of
moving images so that everything can be saved. Unfortunately, there is
also an even more fractious and animated debate in progress on *migration* policies, the need to transfer analog recordings to digital formats,
or digital formats to new digital formats, to meet access requirements,
if not preservation objectives, in the absence of established standards.
With format obsolescence now predicted in months rather than years,
this is another challenge that moving image archivists will face in the
years ahead.

UNESCO's *Recommendation* wisely leaves designation of what
should be deposited, as well as when and how, to national legislation,

but implicit in the *Recommendation* is the concept of selection. I chaired the UNESCO meeting that drafted the *Recommendation* and in 1982 I was asked to conduct a study for the Records and Archives Management Program (RAMP) of UNESCO on the appraisal of moving images published by UNESCO in 1983 as *The Archival Appraisal of Moving Images: A RAMP Study With Guidelines.*

This was the first attempt to examine the principles that should govern the assessment of *archival value* with regard to moving images, an assessment that should be carried out *before* moving images are acquired. Much of the history of the film archive movement in this work was compiled for the *RAMP Study*, and for an update that appeared as appendix D, "Some Observations on Audio-Visual Heritage Programs in Other Countries" in *Fading Away: Strategic Options to Ensure the Protection of and Access to Our Audio-Visual Memory,* published by the National Archives of Canada in 1995.

In recent years determining the *monetary value* of moving images has become an even more contentious issue for all custodial institutions. The introduction of taxation policies that encourage gifts of moving images to archives, museums, and libraries has made the monetary assessment of moving images an essential factor in the management of such institutions. The vast increase in the use of archival footage in contemporary productions, the rapid development of commercial stockshot libraries, and the increasing pressure on custodial institutions to generate revenue by marketing their holdings, has focused attention on the monetary value of even the most innocuous footage and pressured custodians to assess it in terms of potential revenue.

Assessing the monetary value of unique historical documents is even more problematical. The 8mm film taken by Abraham Zapruder at the time John F. Kennedy was assassinated and the legal proceedings surrounding its acquisition by the U.S. National Archives is indicative of the complications inherent in applying dollar value assessments to moving images of "historic" significance. At one point, appraisers for the Zapruder estate and for the U.S. Government were thirty million dollars apart in their estimates of the value of the 8mm film!

The work that follows owes much to the contacts I have had with moving image archivists from all over the world for the past forty years. They have generously shared their experiences (their triumphs *and* their frustrations!) and their thoughts on appraisal. Through my work with the International Federation of Film Archives, the International Federation of Television Archives, the Association of Canadian

Archivists, the International Council on Archives, and through seminars and symposia I have conducted for UNESCO, I have had the opportunity to test these concepts and to benefit from the observations of custodians from many different institutions in many countries. Through my current service on the boards of the Association of Moving Image Archivists (www.amianet.org—777 members in 23 countries at the end of 2001) and the AV Preservation Trust.CA, I am continuing to monitor the evolution of principles and practices that should govern the management of moving image archives in the twenty-first century.

I am also very grateful to my colleagues in what was known as the National Film, Television and Sound Archives of the National Archives of Canada when I directed the division between 1973 and 1989. It was there that I first attempted to formulate principles of appraisal, and through discussions on the selection of other archival media, both textual and nontextual, my colleagues at the Archives contributed immeasurably to my understanding of appraisal principles and policies. Since my retirement, I have had the opportunity to test some of these principles by carrying out archival and monetary appraisals of moving images, and by consulting with the Canadian Cultural Property Export Review Board as they formulated policies and guidelines for the certification of moving images as donations to designated institutions in Canada.

For encouragement and technical support in producing this work I am indebted to my daughters, Helen and Jocelyn. For her patience and understanding I owe my wife Bunty a greater debt of gratitude than I can ever repay.

What follows are essentially my own conclusions on a set of principles on which appraisal policies could be based. There is no broader consensus on appraisal policy with regard to specific documentation in Canada than there is in the larger archival community!

Notes

    * Paraphrased from the opening line of the Fowler Committee on Broadcasting, Report to the Prime Minister of Canada, 1965: "In broadcasting, the only thing that really matters is the quality of the programs; all the rest is housekeeping."

    1. Hilary Jenkinson, *A Manual of Archives Administration* (Oxford: Clarendon Press, 1922); Theodore R. Schellenberg, *Modern Archives: Principles*

and Techniques (Chicago: Society of American Archivists, 1956). For a review of Jenkinson and Schellenberg in the light of contemporary thought on appraisal see Terry Cook, "Mind Over Matter: Towards a New Theory of Archival Appraisal," In *The Archival Imagination: Essays in Honour of Hugh A. Taylor,* ed. Barbara L. Craig. (Ottawa: Association of Canadian Archivists, 1992) 38-70.

2. F. Gerald Ham, "The Archival Edge," In *A Modern Archives Reader,* eds. Maygene F. Daniels and Timothy Walch. (Washington, D.C.: National Archives and Records Service, 1984) 326.

3. For a review of two biographies of Langlois see Sam Kula, "Film Archives at the Centenary of Film," *Archivaria* 40 (fall 1995): 210-225.

Chapter 1

History of Moving Image Archives

That moving images of actual people, places, and events—*actualities*, as they were termed at the turn of the century—are historical documents with unique properties was being recognized as early as 1898. Just two years after the first public exhibitions of cinematography in Paris, London, Berlin, and New York, Boleslaw Matuszewski, a Polish cinematographer in the employ of Nicholas II of Russia, published a manifesto in Paris calling for the establishment of a worldwide network of archives to acquire and conserve the product of this new marvel of technology, this "new source of history."[1] Matuszewski was aware that for cinematography to fulfill its historic mission it would first have to move from "purely recreational or fantastic subjects toward actions and events of *documentary* [my emphasis] interest; from the slice of life as human interest to the slice of life as the cross-section of a nation and a people." In other words the objectives of the cinematographers would have to differ from those of their predecessors who had developed the magic lantern and optical toys, based on the *persistence of vision* and the illusion of motion, to a very sophisticated level as a means of personal or public amusement.

Matuszewski was not naïve, however. He was aware of the cinematographer's limitations, aware that much of what was photographed would be "ceremonies arranged in advance and posed in front of the camera." He conceded that "the camera will not perhaps give us complete history, but at least what it gives us will be incontestable and absolutely true . . . . It has a quality of authenticity, exactitude, and precision that is unique to it. It is the honest and infallible eye witness." Because of this, he argued, "it is necessary to give this source, perhaps a privileged one, the same authority, the same official existence and the same possibilities as the other recognized archives." Matuszewski was, however, also a realist: "I have no illusions that my project will quickly be made effective."

What is remarkable is that Matuszewski also foresaw the eventual need for the appraisal and selection of moving images. One of the functions of the "competent committee" he proposed to administer the *Depository of Historical Cinematography* to be established in Paris was to "accept or reject the proposed documents according to their historic value." He assumed that the volume of voluntary deposits by cinematographers anxious to have their films permanently conserved would demand an appraisal policy. He even had the foresight to predict that as the cost of cameras and projectors came down in price—the *Cinématographe Lumière*, after all, was a camera, a projector, and a means of making copies all in one apparatus—even amateurs would be able record the world around them "and would like nothing better than to contribute to the making of history."

Matuszewski was not alone in promoting the properties of the motion picture camera as an instrument to document a world that is constantly changing. In 1900 the Ethnographic Congress in Paris adopted this resolution:

> All anthropological museums should add suitable film archives to their collections. The mere possession of a potter's wheel, a number of weapons, or a primitive loom is not sufficient for a full understanding of their functional use; this can only be handed down to posterity by means of precise cinematographic records.[2]

Anthropologist and ethnographers were thus among the first to adopt the new technology as an additional tool, along with the still camera and the audio recorder, but there was little systematic coverage of traditional cultures undergoing rapid change. As Francis Speed points out in describing the situation in Nigeria, the irony is that this product of the new technology has not been more widely employed in recording cultures threatened by the introduction of all types of new technology.

> Already many of these cultures have disappeared; their ways of life have basically and irrevocably changed and comparatively few have been reliably and comprehensively documented . . . . In a living culture the majority of the ritual, social, political, and working occupations entail continuous and complex movements. In order to make comprehensive and reliable records of these activities it is necessary to use an audiovisual medium capable of reproducing movement.[3]

Despite the enthusiasms of the few who perceived the new medium of motion pictures to be capable of capturing a unique record of human endeavor in the twentieth century, and despite the almost universal public acceptance of motion pictures, the first mass medium to transcend both international boundaries and cultural differences, the moving images produced were almost totally neglected by librarians, museum curators, and archivists.

In the beginning there were essentially two approaches to film-making as far as the general public was concerned: in the first camp were those, following in the footsteps of Auguste and Louis Lumière, who found their subject matter in the real world around them; in the second camp were those inspired by the fantasies of Georges Méliès, an illusionist turned film-maker, who discovered that the limitations of the real world in terms of time and space could be overcome through the *magic of the movies*, the transformation of real time and real space into screen time and screen space. The initial objective of the filmmakers in both camps, at least in the commercial cinema, was to entertain, to attract an audience to the profit of the producer, the distributor, and the exhibitor. The followers of Méliès proved to be more successful at the box-office, especially after the development of narrative techniques, and the actualities began to play an increasingly minor role in the emerging film industry.

Fact and fiction fused very early in the history of motion pictures as those purporting to be capturing history on the fly started reenacting it when they could not film the real thing. Francis Doublier in Paris was fabricating a film on the Dreyfus affair, and James Williamson in London was simulating an attack on a Chinese Mission during the Boxer Rebellion before the turn of the century.

Moving images quickly became associated with *vulgar entertainment,* the popular culture of the music halls and burlesque theatres with which they were first associated, and the only *value* assigned to them was measured by the financial return they could generate. Although, in numbers, well over half the moving images produced during the first quarter of the twentieth century continued to be actualities—especially after the introduction of newsreels as a standard component of the film program around 1910[4]—the feature length fiction films and the host of short films—comedies, dramatic serials, travelogs—produced by the major studios, *the dream factory,* so dominated the public consciousness that almost all moving images were regarded by the custodians of artifact and culture as escapist fare of no lasting value.

Even as moving images in the twenties and thirties began to be harnessed in the service of national and international ideologies, and as the impact of moving images as shapers of public opinion and molders of public taste began to be recognized by politicians and advertisers alike, there was no concerted effort to systematically acquire and conserve the moving images of one generation for the enjoyment and edification of those to follow. By the end of the silent era in the late twenties there was also widespread appreciation that the fiction film was an art form in its own right, *the seventh art*, but there was still no coordinated effort to protect the works. As a result, it is estimated that fully one-half of the moving images produced before 1930 have been lost, or to be more precise, are not known to exist.

One of the major contributing factors was the nature of the nitro-cellulose stock that was used for all 35mm theatrical productions prior to 1950. Although long wearing and with excellent optical qualities, nitrocellulose is an inherently unstable and flammable compound that gradually disintegrates over time, especially if not stored under climate controlled conditions.[5] It is only in recent years that we have learned that nitrocellulose, or *nitrate stock,* when stored under optimal low-humidity cold storage conditions, will last as long as acetate stock, the so-called *safety* film to which it was copied, and that acetate stock itself is subject to breakdown under poor storage conditions, signaled by the formation of acetic acid, the dreaded *vinegar syndrome.*

The only known method of conserving moving images on nitrate stock for industry purposes prior to 1950 was to transfer the images to fresh stock, and the prospect of having to do this every few years, along with the storage problems associated with highly flammable materials, acted as a powerful deterrent on archives, libraries, and museums that might otherwise have assumed responsibility for what was becoming recognized as a vital part of the public record.

The Library of Congress in the U.S., for example, accepted the deposit of moving images as series of photographs printed on paper rolls for the purpose of copyright registration from 1894 through 1912 and thus acquired an invaluable collection of more than 3,000 pioneer moving image productions. However, when new legislation on copyright in 1912 permitted the deposit of motion pictures as a distinct form of artistic work, the Library, faced with the deposit of nitrate stock prints (the Library never required the deposit of master material), changed its regulations so that the motion pictures were returned to the copyright claimants, with the Library retaining only descriptive printed material relating to them. The Library did not resume the acquisition of moving images (with rare exception) until 1942, and then only for selected works.[6] The criteria shifted over the next twenty years but always focused on historically significant feature films. The Library did not institute the acquisition policy that has now created the largest collection of moving images in the world until the end of the sixties.

It was not until the early thirties, when the introduction of sound had placed all silent films in danger because they were no longer commercially competitive, that the first archives specifically devoted to the acquisition and conservation of moving images were organized. These first archives were founded on the work of individuals, and frequently were based on private collections that were *institutionalized* in order to ensure funds for conservation, control over access, and the continuity of support necessary to enlist the cooperation of depositors.

The earliest successful pioneer was Bengt Idestam Almquist, who established the first film archives in Europe, and arguably the world, in Stockholm in 1933; but the most influential pioneers were Henri Langlois (Cinémathèque Françaises, Paris), Ernest Lindgren (National Film Library, London), and Iris Barry (Museum of Modern Art Film Library, New York). Through the force of their personalities they secured public recognition of the need for moving image archives, and established the legitimacy of their calling[7]

Their approach to building their collections was, however, markedly different, a characteristic that has marked all moving image archives to this day. Rather than being based on any set of common principles, the collecting mandates they developed were essentially a reflection of their character and the institutions to which the moving image archive program was attached.

Langlois was essentially a private collector who institutionalized his "passion for film," focused almost exclusively on the feature film, in 1936, and declared that any policy of selection was an evil that archivists should avoid at all costs.[8] His collection was avowedly international, and while he never turned any film away, he managed to neglect large segments of the French national production. Under his direction the Cinémathèque Françaises allocated most of the resources provided by the French government to public screenings and museum exhibitions, with very little left for the preservation or the conservation program. The result was very inadequate storage facilities, the suspected loss of an unknown number of films (Langlois did not place cataloging the collection as a high priority) while they were in storage, and two major fires that wiped out a significant portion of the collection.

Although he served as Secretary General of the International Federation of Film Archives (FIAF) from 1946 to 1959, Langlois resisted any efforts at coordinating the activities of the member archives beyond the exchange of films to build his collection and to program theatres. He would never have accepted any limitations on his acquisition policy, which was simply to take everything that was offered to him. His quarrels inside FIAF on his autocratic administration of the organization (he stormed out in 1959 and never returned), and with the French government, when they began to demand an accounting of how the subsidies provided to the Cinémathèque Françaises were being used, were as legendary as his appetite for food and for films. In 1968 he was the focus of a remarkable series of street demonstrations against the government when they tried to remove him as director. In 1974 he was awarded an honorary Academy Award, the first and only Oscar an archivist has ever received.

Langlois used his magnificent collection—the story has it that he held 300 feature films at the beginning of WWII and 3000 by the end of the War!—as a resource to assist many other archivists in emerging archives, and he is widely credited with giving *cinematheques* currency as important cultural assets throughout the world. In Penelope Houston's apt epitaph: "He created a legend, gloried in it, and before the end he was its prisoner."[9]

After his death in 1977 the government rationalized the moving image archive situation in France by turning the preservation and conservation responsibility for the national production over to the Centre National de la Cinématographie, which had actually been established as the national archive for moving images in 1968, with the Cinémathèque Françaises continuing with its exhibition and educational programs. The third component in the French national system is the Cinémathètheque de Toulouse, a regional archive with an important collection, especially of the national production of the forties and fifties that had been neglected by Langlois, that had long been overshadowed by Langlois and his archive/theater/museum empire.

Across the channel the national collection began very modestly as the collection of the British Film Institute. The Institute had been established in 1933 with the objective "to encourage the development of the art of the film, to promote its use as a record of contemporary life and manners, and to foster public appreciation and study of it from these points of view."[10] A library of films was a necessity to further the educational aims of the Institute, and in 1935 Ernest Lindgren was given the assignment, as director of the National Film Library, to create "a repository of films of permanent value."[11]

At first the goal was to be comprehensive, based on a system of statutory deposit, much like the legislation that ensured that a copy of every book found its way into the British Library. Lindgren sounded like Langlois when he wrote that "any kind of selective system must be unsatisfactory. *Every* film has a historical value of some kind."[12] Unfortunately, the government was not prepared to enact such legislation over the strenuous objections of the film industry, and with no funds to purchase copies from the producers and distributors, the fledgling library cum archive was, in Lindgren's words "a beggar with nothing to give, a national organization ridiculously dependent on what amounts to the charity of an industry."[13]

Lindgren continued to beg, but the Library had to be very selective in the titles it requested. An elaborate system of selection committees was instituted with experts in science, history, and the art and aesthetics of the film assisting the staff. Ironically, the trickle of films became a unselected flood when the government imposed severe restrictions on the storage of nitrate films in central London in the seventies. The Rank organization alone turned over twenty-five thousand cans.

In sharp contrast to Langlois, Lindgren believed that preservation and conservation should take precedence over exhibition and public access to the collection.

In 1938 four of the pioneer organizations, the Cinémathèque Françaises, the Museum of Modern Art Film Library, the National Film Library, and the Reichsfilmarchiv, Berlin, founded the International Federation of Film Archives (FIAF). World War II interrupted that development, but the Federation was reestablished in 1946 by the archives in Paris, New York, and London, with the addition of Gosfilmofond, Moscow. In 2000 there were 124 affiliated members in 66 countries in the Federation, and although the majority of the full members are from Europe and North America, all continents are represented. It is one of the Federations' chief objectives to assist in the formation and growth of moving image archives in developing countries. There has been significant success in Latin America and Southeast Asia, although many archives are so starved for resources they can barely pay their membership fees; there has been very little progress in Africa.

An analysis of FIAF's membership reveals that very few moving image collections have been established in national archives or libraries. The collections at the National Archives of Canada, the Library of

Congress (U.S.), the National Library of Norway, and the Bundesarchiv (FRG), are notable exceptions. The Federation's Statutes that demand an autonomous structure for the moving image activity as a condition for membership may have deterred other national archives or libraries that do acquire moving images from seeking affiliation. The vast majority of FIAF members and observers in Western Europe, North America and Latin American are autonomous, private organizations, or affiliated with film institutes or film schools. They usually receive governmental financial support directly or indirectly but their policies and programs are developed and implemented by a small professional staff responsible to some type of governing board of directors.

In recent years the film archivists of the European Union have formed their own association to lobby for financial support and to promote development of film preservation and access to film resources. Founded in 1991 as the Association of Film Archivists of the European Union (ACCE), in 1996 they were restructured as the Association of European Cinémathèques (ACE) with 31 members, all remaining full or affiliated members of FIAF. Their major effort is the Lumière Project, the restoration of 1,000 silent films, the search for lost films, and the compilation of a European filmography.[14]

In 1996 as well, a significant regional association of film and video archives was established. The Southeast Asia-Pacific Audiovisual Archives Association (SEAPAVAA) has objectives that mirror those of FIAF. Its formation is indicative of the spread of the movement to conserve the audio-visual heritage that is now worldwide.

Most film archives do not systematically acquire moving images from television, either as film or videotape, although some of the organizations established in recent years (Scottish Film and Television Archive, Glasgow; Wales Film and Television Archive, Aberystwyth; National Library of Norway, Mo) collect moving images from any source. In recent years some long-established film archives have extended their collecting mandate to include television (La Cinémathèque Québécoise, Montreal; National Film and Television Archive of the British Film Institute, London) and some have incorporated all moving images for many years (Library of Congress, Washington; National Archives of Canada, Ottawa; UCLA Film and Television Archive, Los Angeles; ScreenSound, Canberra). Because so much of television broadcasting, as introduced in the early fifties, was direct transmission or *live,* there was no permanent record to select and acquire, and the film recordings (kinescopes) that were manufactured to allow the retransmission of certain broadcasts at a more convenient time were either ignored or allowed to accumulate in the offices of the producers and junked when the space was required for other purposes.

As broadcast television became a great consumer of film, either produced for television or purchased for broadcast, more and more news film, documentaries, and fiction films ended up on the shelves of the networks or in local station libraries, usually closed to the public and frequently neglected in terms of organization and conservation, so that the material could not even serve effectively as a resource for the broadcaster.

With the introduction of videotape in the early sixties a record of what was broadcast could be retained for archive purposes, but in fact very few broadcasts left the hands of the producers for research or record purposes. Worse still, the cost of the raw stock videotape combined with the fact that it could be erased and reused led to the loss of thousands of hours of programming. In short, the archival history of the first twenty-five years of television broadcasting throughout the world replicated the dismal history of film production in its first fifty years. The documentation, when it survived, remained in the hands of the producers and distributors, whose mandate seldom included conservation or organization for public access.

By the mid-seventies, however, the value of archived television broadcasts, and the raw material acquired for the broadcasts as a future production resource, was becoming well established, and the importance of television broadcasting as an integral part of the public record was increasingly recognized by researchers in many disciplines. The response from the television producers was to re-evaluate and in many cases to reorganize their production resources as archives, accepting the fact that even internally the programs and program elements had to be protected from indiscriminate and irresponsible use due to the always pressing demands of the broadcast schedule.

At the same time academically orientated bodies such as the International Association for Media and History (IAMHIST), the Association for the Study of Canadian Radio and Television (Canada), and the British Universities Film and Video Council (U.K.), the Society for Cinema Studies (U.S.), and organizations of archivists (Association of Moving Image Archivists) began focusing attention on the need to conserve the record of television broadcasting and to organize the resources for at least limited public access by researchers.

In the United States the 1976 Copyright Act established the Ameri-

can Television and Radio Archive at the Library of Congress. This
formalized the inclusion of works made for television in the Library's
acquisition policy. In recent years the Library has promoted the necessity of a national program for the preservation of television involving
both public institutions and the broadcasters themselves. The first step
was a study on the current state of television and video preservation,
which reported in 1997. One of its chief recommendations was the establishment of a national television preservation board that would parallel the work of the national film preservation board set up in 1996.[15]

In 1978, primarily through the initiative of Institut National de
L'Audiovisuel (Paris), the British Broadcasting Corporation (London),
Radiotelevisione Italiana (Rome), and Norddeutsher Rundfunk Fernse-
hen (Hamburg), the archives of the major television networks throughout the world established the International Federation of Television
Archives (FIAT). Membership was restricted at first to archives of production organizations, or to those media archives that have been officially designated as the archives of a television network or production
company, such as the National Film and Television Archive (London)
for Independent Broadcasting Authority companies. Membership is
now open to all organizations seriously engaged in the long-term preservation of television.

There are over 115 members and associate members in FIAT, with
the membership concentrated in Western Europe. The conditions that
prevail in almost all other state television networks (the norm for television broadcasting through the world) is similar, in that archives, if
they exist as functional entities, remain the responsibility of the producer. In some cases this responsibility has been delegated to a national
library (as in Sweden, Norway, and the U.S.), but this is still rare, although changes in technology that reduce the volume of storage required for the selective retention of the records of broadcasting organizations may make these programs viable models for other countries.

With the exceptions noted above, the involvement of national archives in the selection and conservation of television broadcasts is
minimal. Substantially less, in fact, than with moving image documents
from other sources, even though the technology associated with preservation and public service on videotape recordings was actually less
complicated and less costly when videotape was first introduced in the
sixties than it was with early film. The deterrent initially was volume
and the perception that most of what was broadcast was ephemeral,
repetitive, or both. It is not unusual for a single broadcaster to generate

over 5000 hours of programs per year. The deterrent now is the rapid obsolescence of video recording formats and the need to transfer from one format to another at very significant costs.

Network archives now regard their holdings as *assets* and they are engaged in *asset management*, a term that implies both protection and the effective exploitation of the resources for internal and external markets. Selection is still a necessity: no network retains every hour that is broadcast in the form that it was originally transmitted, complete with advertisements. What is needed is, in effect, a record management program that will ensure the immediate protection of all the records generated for a limited time, to allow time for an evaluation of the total production for archival purposes and the preparation of a schedule which will specify which programs are to be retained for long-term preservation. This is the stated objective of the network archives that are members of FIAT. These recommendations will be discussed in chapter 4.

The Institut National de l'Audiovisuel has established a very elaborate and effective program for all television broadcasting in France, but the norm for television archives that are not actually part of the production organization is a much more selective approach based on advisory committees and consultation with subject experts. Since so much of television's output consists of films that may also have been or will be available through theatrical distribution, there is obviously a large potential overlap with the work of film archives. Television, worldwide, is also a rapacious consumer of theatrical feature films and documentaries. In many countries the television broadcasters acquired news film libraries to ensure rapid access to visual resources. The separation of moving images by delivery mechanisms (television versus theatrical distribution) for archives purposes may thus be wasteful of public resources, with the potential for dividing the work of one image-maker between two archives that may well be in different cities.

The degree to which archives in television networks can serve and should serve the general public of scholars and researchers is also an issue. Indicative of the nature of the problem is the Report of the Advisory Committee on Archives, established by the British Broadcasting Corporation (BBC) in 1978. Although recommending that the BBC's archives should be made more accessible to outside researchers and the general public through in-house services and various diffusion policies, the Report recognizes that additional funding will have to be allocated to allow the archives to both serve the network and this wider public. The Report proposed what was seen as an interim solution; the BBC would deposit selected programs in the National Film and Television Archives and underwrite the Archive's costs of providing public access. A similar arrangement was implemented in Sweden, with the National Library providing the public service.

In recent years, as the tape recorder became a ubiquitous witness to public events and private conversations, archives at the national, regional, and local level have been increasingly acquiring recorded sound as a component of other accessions, whether public records or private papers. In much the same way, film and video recordings are proliferating in archival record or manuscript groups. It is probably safe to say that the annual accession list of every national archive would show some intake of moving image and recorded sound, whether or not the archive officially subscribes to a *total archive* acquisition policy.

How this type of documentation is treated, however, once it enters the archival system, varies widely. The range is from a policy that can be termed *benign neglect*, the passive registration and shelving of the object along with the textual material in the same record group or collection, to an active policy of preservation and public service that not only recognizes that such documentation must be segregated physically to protect the recordings (and, in the case of film on nitrocellulose stock, the repository itself!), but also that such documentation must be described in greater detail, perhaps item by item, than is probably the norm in a national archives, to make them readily accessible to researchers.

Despite the best efforts of commissions in FIAF, FIAT, and UNESCO's International Film and Television Council that have attempted to standardize the cataloging of moving images, little has been accomplished beyond some movement toward a definition of terminology and an acceptable list of minimal data elements. These organizations, together with the International Federation of Library Associations (IFLA) and the International Association of Sound Archives (IASA) continue to collaborate in joint efforts at standardization, with limited success. This effort is now directed by UNESCO's Coordinating Council of Audiovisual Archives Associations that is also concerned with technological change and how moving image archives must respond to the challenges of digital communications in all formats.

In North America there appears to be greater prospects for success in developing cataloging standards through the integration of the Rules for Archival Description, developed by the Canadian Council on Archives, and the rules for Archives, Personal Papers and Manuscripts, developed by the Society of American Archivists. This will establish a common standard that will incorporate rules for the description of audiovisual holdings. Whether the wide variety of organizations and institutions now engaged in moving image preservation will adopt such a standard remains to be seen.

In practice archivists in production organizations, such as television networks, tend to more detail in describing their holdings in order to meet the needs of their colleagues in production who may request highly specific shots or sequences. This approach is beyond the capacity of more general collections—in fact, television archives tend to reserve this treatment for news film—but there is little general agreement as to what constitutes an acceptable compromise. When one considers that one minute of a motion picture, measured at sound speed, contains 1,440 photographs, some of the problems involved can be appreciated. In order to cope with the volume of data generated through this type of analysis, many of the television archives have already adopted machine-readable cataloging systems, or are experimenting with computerized retrieval systems. The facility to rapidly exchange data on holdings should accelerate the move toward standardization. The growing recognition that the addition of metadata (even if restricted to *tombstone*, or very basic data) to every production, given the technology that will permit this, will greatly facilitate its future use is also promoting standardization.

The UNESCO Recommendation concerning the safeguarding and preservation of moving images, as adopted by the General Assembly in Belgrade, October 1980, called for the establishment of officially recognized archives "by each member state to acquire and preserve all moving images of national production . . . considered by Member States as an integral part of their 'moving image heritage'." The *Recommendation* foresees a mix of governmental and nongovernmental archives as achieving this objective in some countries, particularly where such non-governmental archives already exist. The *Recommendation* will be discussed in detail in chapter 4.

The existence of the *Recommendation* is an acknowledgment of a worldwide concern that moving images are a part of our global cultural heritage, in every sense of that term, which has already suffered extensive damage through neglect and acts of deliberate destruction. All custodial institutions will inevitably be called upon to play a larger role in assuring that this aspect of the historic record will be conserved, but whether this will be an active role or merely one of coordination and the establishment of standards may well vary with circumstances from country to country. Certainly in countries where there is no institutionalized effort to acquire and conserve moving images at present, there is a strong argument for national archives to assume that responsibility, or at least to ensure that this responsibility is delegated to an organization serving the public interest.

Notes

1. Boleslaw Matuszewski, *Une Nouvelle Source de l'histoire: Creation d'un Dépot de Cinématographie Historique,* (Paris: 1898).

2. Francis Speed, "The Function of the Film as Historical Record." *African Notes* 6, (1968): 46.

3. Speed, "Film as Historical Record," 49.

4. Raymond Fielding, *The American Newsreel 1911-1967* (Norman, Oklahoma: University of Oklahoma Press, 1972: 69.

5. International Federation of Film Archives (FIAF), *A Handbook for Film Archives* (Brussels: FIAF, 1980); Sam Kula, "Mea Culpa: How I Abused the Nitrate in My Life." *The Moving Image* 1 (Spring 2001): 198-202.

6. Doug Herrick, "Toward a National Film Collection: Motion Pictures at the Library of Congress." *Film Library Quarterly* 13, (1980): 5-25.

7. Raymonde Borde, *Les Cinémathèques,* (Paris: Editions L/Age d'Homme, 1983); Sam Kula, "Film Archives at the Centenary of Film," *Archivaria* 40 (Fall 1995): 210-25.

8. Richard Roud, *A Passion for Films: Henri Langlois and the Cinémathèque Française,* (New York: Viking Press, 1983); Glenn Myrent and George P. Langlois, *Henri Langlois: First Citizen of Cinema,* (New York: Twayne, 1995).

9. Penelope Houston, *Keepers of the Frame: The Film Archives,* (London: British Film Institute, 1994) 49.

10. Ivan Butler, *"To Encourage the Art of the Film": The Story of the British Film Institute,* (London: Robert Hale, 1971).

11. Houston, *Keepers of the Frame,* 25.

12. Houston, *Keepers of the Frame,* 27.

13. Houston, *Keepers of the Frame,* 34.

14. *The Lumière Project: The European Archives at the Crossroads* Catherine A. Surowiec, ed. (Lisbon: ACCE, 1996).

15. Librarian of Congress, *Television and Video Preservation 1997: A Report on the Current State of American Television and Video Preservation,* (Washington, D.C.: Library of Congress, 1997).

Chapter 2

Appraisal Theory

Appraisal of documentation for long-term conservation has always been a controversial element in archival theory and practice. With the advent of electronic records and the prospect of record management in a post-custodial era, appraisal has become even more of a bellwether for archival theory. Whether it is characterized as science or intuition, there is the presumption that a system of values underlies what archivists do that differentiates them from anyone else collecting documentation, and that appraisal—the assessment of archival value—is part of that system.

In the last decade, appraisal has become one of the central topics in archival literature. To judge by the literature in English, it appears in the minds of many archivists to be shifting from a means to an end, essentially acquisition, to a central place in archival theory.[1] Appraisal, in the sense the term is normally used by North American archivists, refers to the assessment of records for the purpose of determining whether or not the records should be acquired. Luciana Duranti makes the important distinction that appraisal is actually "the attribution of value to archival material, and not the act of selection or acquisition of archival material."[2] In general use appraisal can refer to both the assessment of the documentation in relation to its *monetary* (or *fair market*, or *intrinsic*) value, or to its *archival* value (historical, informational, research) in relation to the society supporting the archival activity, now and in the future. The two approaches should, of course, relate to each other. That they frequently do not is an additional complication, particularly in countries in which donations of documentation can result in benefits to the donor as a result of tax legislation.[3] The assessment of the monetary value of moving images is considered in chapter 6.

Appraisal of the archival value of moving image documentation is even more contentious. Because the documents can seldom be categorized as functional or evidentiary with relation to the activities of the

agency that created them, appraisal inevitably involves selection because of the costs involved in processing and long-term storage, and
moving images tend to be assessed on an item-by-item basis. At the
risk of pressing the obvious, appraisal without selection, without either
the scheduling for destruction of documents not selected, or the decision to acquire and protect certain documents while others available to
the archives are allowed to self-destruct in the hands of the creator or
creating agency, is hardly a critical issue. If everything that is identified
is eventually accessioned then appraisal remains nothing more than the
first phase of acquisition, with the addition, possibly, of a written justification that would only be challenged by financial comptrollers concerned about processing and storage costs, and by researchers required
to sift through too much chaff in order to locate the kernels.

Whatever the approach to appraisal, archival literature offers little
in the way of concrete and practical guidance. Archival theorists have
been wringing their hands over this critical gap for many years. Theodore Schellenberg, writing in 1956, had to concede: "Archivists of different archival institutions may . . . use different criteria in evaluating
similar types of records, for what is valuable to one archival institution
may be valueless to another."[4] In 1975 Gerald Ham lamented: "Is there
any other field of information gathering that has such a broad mandate
with a selection process so random, so fragmented, so uncoordinated,
and even so accidental?"[5] Margaret Hedstrom concluded in 1989 that
"there are no guidelines of professional standards for reaching appraisal
decisions or documenting the decision making process."[6] A standard-
ized and controlled vocabulary to describe the factors that archivists
should consider in the appraisal process would be an important contribution, but even that is lacking. As Terry Eastwood observed in 1992,
"there has been plenty of thinking by archivists about appraisal, but no
theory of appraisal has yet been expounded such that it is generally accepted as the foundation of methodology and practice."[7]

Hedstrom and Eastwood were primarily concerned with government records. There has been less thought on appraisal theory in relation to moving images and even less effect of theory on practice. As the
brief survey of moving images and archives presented in chapter 1 in-
dicates, national archives largely ignored moving images, and the archivists in nongovernmental organizations that were established to protect moving images usually had no formal archival training, were
seldom members of professional associations of archivists, and rarely
contributed to archival journals.

The basic principles that underpin any appraisal policy, however, serve all media equally well. These principles are not immutable but they should endure longer than selection standards or criteria that should, in any case, be revised every five years and rewritten every generation, in much the same way, and for many of the same reasons, that each generation of historians reinterprets history.

For modern archivists working in English, and concerned only with archival value, appraisal can be defined as "the process of determining the value and thus the disposition of records based upon their current administrative, legal, and fiscal use; their evidential and informational or research value; their arrangement; and their relationship to other records."[8] This was, to some extent, re-stated as the purpose of appraisal standards by the experts who were consulted on the development of UNESCO's *Records and Archive Management Programme* (RAMP) in 1979:

> To ensure the appraisal by archival services of these noncurrent records and the transfer to adequately equipped repositories for permanent preservation of those that have value and usefulness as basic evidence of the origin, structure, functions, procedures, and significant transactions of the institution that created or received and used them in the conduct of its business, or that contains unique information of value for historical or other research or reference purposes.[9]

The key word in both the definition and the statement of purpose is, of course, *value*. Archivists do not merely identify value, they also create value when they attribute it to a document and then complete the accession, and they destroy it when they sentence a document (or an entire series of documents) to destruction[10], just as they create memory by their selection of records on behalf of the community they serve. However, as Jane Turner, argued in her thesis on the theory of appraisal for selection, "value is a relative term . . . and should only be used when a perspective is involved, such as the perspective of an administrator, researcher or archivist."[11] Or as Terry Cook observed, "values are not found in records, but rather in theories of value of societal significance which archivists bring to records."[12]

The concept of appraisal, the need for selection as an archival function did not emerge in archive theory until the end of the eighteenth century although the underlying principles (authenticity, reliability, and unbroken custody) were developed in the Roman Empire.[13] In his *Modern Archives: Principles and Techniques*, Schellenberg traces the history of appraisal standards to France and the establishment of the first national archival institution in 1789. Faced with the accumulated records that documented the legal, fiscal, and political activities of institutions that had been swept away by the Revolution, the decree of 25 June 1794, established a special committee (Bureau de triage) to sort the surviving records into classes. Those that were useful in documenting government claims to expropriated properties were to be retained. Those that were deemed historical (Chartes et Monument appartenant a l'histoire, aux science et aux art) were also conserved. All others, including all those classed as *feudal* in relation to pre-revolutionary rights and privileges, were to be destroyed.[14]

The losses that occurred as a result of this draconian measure, and through the actions of numerous ill-advised commissions that followed in the nineteenth century, led to the promulgation of rigid rules regarding the destruction of public property. In the ordinance approved by the Minister of Public Instruction 1 July 1921, a systematic approach to appraisal is indicated in which elimination is to be "considered as exceptional." All documents that have an historic interest are to be "preserved indefinitely" and all documents created before 1830 (Article 52) are to be included in that category. This concept of establishing a date and then restricting appraisal and selection to documents created after that date was embodied in a number of articulated appraisal guidelines published in the last hundred years. In Germany the date was 1700, in England 1750, in Austria 1815, in France 1830, in Italy, and in the United States 1861.

In 1901, H. O. Meissner, former head of the Prussian Privy State Archives, presented a set of maxims on appraisal that greatly influenced archival theory and were embodied in the first great work on the subject in English.[15] The first maxim was that "old age is to be respected," a declaration that recognized the obvious connection between scarcity and value; that the records of the past tend to diminish in volume the further back in time the archivist penetrates

Meissner appealed for moderation in developing appraisal policies, "extremes are to be avoided," and argued that due consideration was to be given to the source of the documents to be appraised. The documents were obviously not created in a vacuum, and should, therefore, not be assessed without an analysis that included the structure of the organization or administrative unit that created the records and the nature of its activities. Concern for the protection of provenance in the traditional archival literature translated itself into guidelines that argued for the appraisal of entire blocks of records (record groups, series, or files) rather than an item-by-item selection. While this was obviously sound practical advice on retention, it could lead to regrettable losses on disposal if significant individual files (the employment record of a famous artist, for example) were not selected. It was also largely inapplicable to audiovisual records that were generally accessioned and processed item-by-item.

Some archival theorists argued that triage, or selection, while evidently necessary, should be the responsibility of the administrators directly involved in generating the documents in the first place. Hilary Jenkinson held that this reduction should take place before the documents reached the archives, and that it was the archivist's task to conserve *all* the records entrusted to the archives. Only in their totality would the records adequately represent the activities of the administrative units that produced them. Moreover, because records are created as a means for, and a by-product of, action, not "in the interest or for the information of Posterity," and because they are "free from the suspicion of prejudice in regard to the interests in which we now use them," archival documents are impartial and "cannot tell . . . anything but the truth."[16] A noble sentiment, but we now know that the truth the documents convey can be and frequently has been doctored by those in whose custody they rest before being transferred to the archives, either by removing documents or by altering the documents themselves. In dealing with moving images, production by production, the archivist frequently has no choice but to accept the copy held by the last custodian, somewhere in the distribution/exploitation chain, a copy that may be considerably different from the version originally released.

Luciana Duranti adds a very important footnote when discussing Jenkinson's statement:

Impartiality is a characteristic of archival documents, not of their creators, who are naturally partial to their own interests. To protect the impartiality of archives is to protect their capacity to reveal the biases and idiosyncrasies of their creators. This is why it is so difficult to guarantee the appropriate maintenance of current and semi-current documents by their creators, be they organizations or individuals. It cannot be done without alerting them to their document's inherent value, but if creators are made too vividly aware of the power of their documents, they may begin to draw or alter them for the benefit of posterity, and the documents would not be the unselfconscious residue of action but a conscious reflection on it.[17]

This observation should have considerable resonance for moving image archivists faced with DVD versions of important feature films that purport to be the director's "final cut" or "restored" version.

Impartiality was one of characteristics that Jenkinson ascribed to archival documents. Another key characteristic was interrelationship, that every archival document is closely related "to others both inside and outside the group in which it is preserved and . . . its significance depends on these relations."[18] This is a relationship that arises at the moment of creation and significantly affects the meaning of the document and the role it plays in carrying out the intentions of its creator. This is an important factor in assessing the value of moving images produced as a series for television or as part of a coordinated production program. Paradoxically, each document is at the same time unique, even if it appears to be identical to another document. To push this point to an extreme, if five copies are printed from the same negative at the same time there will still be differences among them because of the chemistry involved in processing and the wear on the negative. Anyone attempting to select the *best* print from among three or more used prints of a feature film can attest to the uniqueness of each print.

One other characteristic of archives that Jenkinson described, *authenticity*, has a bearing on the assessment of moving images. Authenticity is linked to the continuum of creation, maintenance, and custody. If a film or video has been in the unbroken custody of its creator there is prima facie evidence that it is the version that the creator intended for public consumption. The more frequently the custodial role has changed, the more likely it is that the version in hand is not the authentic version.

Jenkinson's influential work, *A Manual of Archives Administration* (1922) was republished in 1937, but the exigencies of World War II caused his colleagues in the U.K. to abandon the theory of *non-evaluation* in favor of a more pragmatic approach to record conservation. Paper had to be salvaged and the Public Record Office began to apply the appraisal principles of the British Records Association, developed for private industry, to public records. These guidelines, unequivocally entitled *Principles Governing the Elimination of Ephemeral or Unimportant Documents in Public or Private Archives*, delineated two broad classes of public records that should be permanently retained in archives: records that document the history and the activities of the originating agency; and records that coincidentally meet potential scholarly needs. In order to drastically reduce the volume of current records the guidelines urged the regular elimination of routine procedural documents, "purely ephemeral," and the introduction of sampling techniques, or at least the retention of specimens selected for their representative character.[19]

In pursuing the principles of appraisal for American archivists and for a generation of archivists who adopted his *Modern Archives: Principles and Techniques* (first published in 1956) as a basic text in archival training, Schellenberg divided all records into two broad groups: *evidential*, in that the records informed on the organization and function of the administrative entity that produced them; and *informational*, in that the records informed on people, places, conditions, and events, in the society in which the administrative entities functioned.[20] In assessing these records Schellenberg was prepared to rely on the *diverse judgments* of professional archivists, an open approach that has been misinterpreted by some as *absolute license* for selection by instinct.

Schellenberg was building on the work of Philip Brooks[21] and Philip Bauer[22] (both staff members of the National Archives and Records Administration in Washington) in attempting to define the evidentiary value of modern records; in approaching the volume of twentieth century records, he stressed the importance of Bauer's observation that the values of records must be weighed against "costs of their preservation." Subsequent commentators on the appraisal of contemporary records such as Brichford,[23] Fishbein,[24] and Pinkett[25] have emphasized the pragmatic factors in appraisal policy. In Brichford's view the "practical world of budget and space" requires the archivist to weigh his financial resources against the prospective usefulness of the records being appraised.

Whether you agree with Jenkinson or not, the question, in Terry Eastwood's words, cannot be avoided: "If archivists are to evaluate archives, can they make their appraisals objective, or must they admit that they are *chained to their biases* . . . and face the consequences of the relative nature of appraisal?"[26] Jenkinson was adamant that "any *conscious* selection is improper"[27] and publicly opposed Schellenberg's proposed attributions of value, evidential and informational, as a guide to acquisition. At the first International Congress of Archives in 1950, Jenkinson restated his total theoretical opposition to appraisal:

> For the Archivist to destroy a document because he thinks it useless is to import into the collection under his charge what we have been throughout most anxious to keep out of it, an element of his personal judgment . . . but for an Administrative body to destroy what it no

longer needs is a matter entirely within its competence and an action
which future ages . . . cannot possibly criticize as illegitimate or as af-
fecting the status of the remaining archives; provided always that the
Administration proceeds only upon those grounds upon which alone it
is competent to make a decision—the needs of its own practical business; provided that is, that it can refrain for thinking of itself as a body
producing historical evidence.[28]

It is difficult today to accept that an administrative body has the
right to destroy what it "no longer needs" even with the proviso, a large
one, that it refrain from thinking of its records as "historical evidence."
In an era when freedom of information and public accountability of
both government and corporate entities are leading issues, it is doubtful
that this approach would be acceptable to many archivists. In fact, in
the aftermath of WWII, and the immense expansion of government
files that accompanied the increasing intervention of the state in all aspects of civil society, even Jenkinson had to concede that archivists
should develop standards of value, even if the principles on which they
were based were not universally acknowledged, as it was no longer
possible to accept all the records that the creating agencies considered
non-current. As a word of comfort to those now responsible for appraisal, Jenkinson urged that later generations of archivists should not
second guess the appraisal decisions of previous ones: "In a word, we
can criticize the past only if it failed to live up to its own standards of
value."[29]

In assessing records for their informational value the basic premise
was that there was a close relationship between documents of continuing relevance to the agency that created them and continuing research
significance; that there is an affinity between the purposes of creators
and of archivists in the service of the research community. Schellenberg's pragmatic approach to appraisal even defined *archives* as a spe-
cies of *records* with the main difference being that archives "must be
preserved for reasons other than those for which they were created or
accumulated."[30] Many appraisal theorists have problems with a definition of archives that implies that the primary reason records must be
preserved is for reasons beyond the intentions of the creators. They
would argue that records must first be preserved as evidence of the actions of the creators. Future research use is a secondary reason. Jenkinson accepted the importance of the use factor, but insisted that appraisal
theory must be based on the analysis of the nature of the documents:

Value for Research is no doubt the reason why we continue to spend time and money on preserving Archives and making them available: but the fact that a thing may be used for purposes for which it was not intended—a hat, for instance, for the production of a rabbit—is not part of its nature and should not, I submit, be made an element of its definition, though it may reasonably affect its treatment. [31]

There is a middle ground between the Jenkinson and Schellenberg positions that Margaret Cross Norton and others have described,[32] although commentators like Felix Hull have pointed out that it is not comfortable ground for many archivists:

You and I by our involvement are either destroying or agreeing to the destruction of that very evidence which, in an almost Hippocratic oath sense, we are professionally bound to defend and preserve. That, without any question, is our first pitfall—a schizophrenic dilemma that we feel would not face us in an ideal world.[33]

For most moving image archivists it is far from an ideal world, and most are searching for a middle ground between the positions adopted by Langlois—take everything you can get, indiscriminately—and by Lindgren—select very carefully for quality to build as representative a collection as possible. Despite the complaints of textual archivists, it is far easier to select on evidentiary value than on informational value. All recorded information has some continuing value to the record creators and to society; the problem, as Margaret Cross Norton observed, is that "it is comparatively easy to select records of permanent value, relatively easy to decide on those of no value. The great bulk of records are borderline."[34]

Unlike the entrenched and contradictory positions adopted by moving image archivists, there is almost total agreement among textual archivists that some reduction in the volume of public records is necessary, and that archival appraisal, no matter how faulty, is preferable to reduction by accident, or random loss, or through partial aggregation that damages provenance and the historical record. Even with the tentative and tendentious formulations on appraisal theory there are no examples of archival appraisal decisions leading to the destruction of documents that were needed "for our protection, development, and intellectual growth."[35]

Richard Cox, among other writers on appraisal theory, has stressed the importance of the user perspective. He quotes the opening pages of

Maynard Brichford's *Archives and Manuscripts: Appraisal and Accessioning:* "The surest proof of sound records appraisal lies in the quality of the archives and the growth of its reputation among the administrators and scholars it serves."[36] The danger is that while archivists may meet the demands of contemporary researchers, they will leave future scholars with a distorted record that will meet neither their needs nor the needs of society in general. Gerald Ham warned that if archivists cannot step back from the academic marketplace in the reliance on actual or anticipated research use as criteria for selection, "the archives will remain at best nothing more than a weathervane moved by the changing winds of historiography."[37]

Moving image archivists collecting film as art rather than record face similar problems in freeing themselves from the accepted canon of great works now the subject of study in the universities. These films, more often than not, are simply the works that have been accessible for academic research in the past quarter century. Because they are acknowledged by scholars as important works, and are by established *auteurs,* copies of these titles, even inferior copies, tend to receive priority for preservation, exhibition, and restoration if necessary. They represent a fraction of the films that are now held in archives, and an even smaller fraction of the films that are still held in private hands.

Terry Eastwood, in an attempt to discern a philosophy of archives that would underwrite appraisal theory, argued that while "we can *deduce* theory from an analysis of ideas, we must *induce* appraisal decisions, because appraisal is essentially predictive, a best guess at what will be valuable."[38] Not very firm ground. As Bauer pointed out in 1946, "prophecy is suspect."[39] Eastwood is aware of the dangers and quotes Schellenberg's solemn observation that "determining importance is somewhat imponderable."[40]

A focus on use tends to revolve around *pertinence,* the relevance a document has to the function and activities of the creating agency, and/or its deemed significance from a political, social, or cultural perspective and, therefore, its value as a resource for research. In assessing moving image productions, pertinence can also concern the relationship of the work in question to the creator's entire output, the production program of the corporate entity responsible, or to the impact the work had on its public and on other image-makers.

Boles and Young suggested that sociological and psychological literature on decision-making might help eliminate hidden biases in the selection process: "Understanding how people behave when they make risky decisions, how they edit, evaluate, and display data, and frame both questions and solutions all has a direct and significant impact on how archivists select information."[41] This may be so, but knowing this is unlikely to be of much help. Archivists are a long way from practical guidelines when the conclusion is that while "conscious selection policymaking is preferable to the more serendipitous alternatives employed by many archivists" archivists will have to accept that "as beauty is in the eye of the beholder, so too historical value is in the eye of the archivist, who must discern it in light of the mission and collecting policy of his or her repository."[42]

One of the biases that therapy might expose, a bias that is reinforced by functional analyses of the agencies creating the records, is a tendency to concentrate on the hierarchical status of the position generating the record as a guide to selection. This results in a *top-down* approach to selection that has come under fire in recent years. Archivists are accused of documenting the actions/lives of the *elites* in society, rather than that of ordinary people, of contributing to the *official* record. Even when those marginalized by society, by reason of race, color, or economic status are documented, the focus is on the elites, the leaders of those communities! Documenting the commonplace may be difficult, but it should remain one of the objectives of *total archives*, a collection that completely represents, in all media, all aspects of political, economic, social, and cultural life in the community the archives serves.

The effort to redress this emphasis on top-down appears to have collided with the recent introduction of *macro-appraisal* theory. It proposes that a functional analysis of an entire department of government, or an entire corporate entity, be conducted *before* any appraisal decisions at the *micro-appraisal* level are implemented. Although this approach appears to offer advantages in dealing with large volumes of public records, and it need not reinforce the tendency to concentrate on the records of the most powerful officials in society, it does little to democratize the process and it has little applicability to the appraisal of moving images.

The effort to develop a *bottom-up* approach has given rise to the concept of *documentation strategy*, a systematic survey of the community the archives serves to ensure that the acquisitions of the archives adequately reflect the diversity of the community.[43] What this approach signals to moving image archivists is the need to move outside the boundaries of the moving image industries to reach out to amateur and independent image-makers, all types of artists working in film and video, and image-making on the margins of society, to ensure that their collections are truly reflective of the entire society.

There is, of course, a cost involved, both at the appraisal stage, and, as always, at the processing and storage stages. For the moving image archivist, the practical obstacles to universal retention are simply insurmountable. Cost is one of the factors that moving image archivists, even those working in very large and very well funded government institutions, can never really forget. The costs involved in the conservation of a moving image document (for example a combined optical print of a 30-minute black-and-white film on 35mm nitrocellulose stock) over a period of 10 years may easily be 100 times the cost of conserving a cubic foot of paper records. As the world moves into a digital mode in all communications the archivist must look forward to transferring the collection again and again to new formats adopted for industry and consumer use. A rigid cost-benefit analysis based on projected use of the film in the next ten or twenty years might argue strongly against the retention of what appears to be a work of limited immediate value. Yet the work may be of great value in documenting an aspect of the social or cultural life of the community the archive serves, and documenting it in a manner that cannot be duplicated by any other type of record.

As has been indicated, archival literature provides little guidance for the appraisal of moving images. The standard manuals by Schellenberg and Jenkinson ignore moving images as an archival resource, although the *Manuel d'archivistique* does contain a section on moving images and recorded sound that examines the grouping of film into three broad categories (oeuvres dramatiques, oeuvres artistique, documents d'historiques) and then, unfortunately, suggests that only *historic films* belong in an archives. In formulating a practical definition of historic for moving image archivists, however, the authors conclude that not only do actualities qualify (films dealing with real people, real places, real events), but that fiction films that reflect the manners, mores, and language of the society that produced them qualify as well. This tends to make a mockery of the initial categorization, as such an interpretation could embrace all moving images, particularly when the impact of the images in relation to the mass audience they attracted is considered.[44]

Because of the way in which moving images are produced and distributed throughout the world, the end products, the images themselves, seldom have evidentiary value. The related documentation—production files, financial and personnel records, contracts and correspondence—may reveal how the production company or administrative entity (whether it be Warner Bros. or the National Film Board of Canada) functioned, but the value of the end product, while it may speak volumes as to the producer's purpose, is primarily informational.

Films and videos are evidential primarily when they are part of a larger campaign to inform and/or persuade a mass audience to a particular point of view or to a particular pattern of behavior. Whether the agency responsible is against the regulation of firearms, or pro-life, or antismoking, the images they disseminate are a direct result of their activities and are evidence of their purpose and policies. This is obvious when the mass media have been harnessed in the service of a totalitarian state. To a critical viewer, however, the advertisements that flood commercial television are just as clearly evidence of the corporate agenda in a capitalist society, and in many ways the subtexts of the programs, as well as that of the *commercials,* are as indicative of the real objectives of the sponsors as anything that might be found in the rest of the corporate archives.[45]

Unfortunately there has been very little consideration of the archival value of a moving image, in terms of its informational or historic significance, in the literature on moving image archives, sparse as that has been, and the approach in the library literature has been restricted to assessments in terms of client needs (primarily educational level and pedagogic soundness) or objectivity of treatment.

There are, for example, only three pages in the International Federation of Film Archives (FIAF) manual, *A Handbook for Film Archives,* dealing with appraisal. The Federation's position, at least in 1980, was that "every archive must develop its own criteria for acquiring films." The Federation, however, did recommend the formulation of a selection policy to guide the archives in appraising collections. These policy statements, it is suggested, could specify the archival objectives in building collections, the types of moving images to be selected in relation to the sources, the physical format in which the images are to be acquired, and the areas in which the archive will attempt to be comprehensive or representative.[46] By 1980 the Federation's members had accepted the fact that no one archive could embrace the world of film, and they had both contributed to and generally agreed with the *Recommendation for the Safeguarding and Preservation of Moving Images* adopted by UNESCO that year. This important document will be discussed in chapter 4.

The International Federation of Television Archives (FIAT), perhaps because most of its members were more homogeneous in character (archives attached to television production organization) adopted a much more detailed set of acquisition standards in January 1981. *Recommended Standards and Procedures for Selection and Preservation of Television Programme Material*, which was revised in September 1996, provides a working guide to the appraisal of television—the broadcasts themselves, and the film, videotape, and audiotape production elements that were the raw materials for the broadcasts.[47] This document will also be discussed in chapter 4.

Translating theory into practice, especially when the theory is so nebulous, has been a challenge that moving image archives have tended to tackle in their own way, and with mixed results.

In June 1980, the International Federation of Film Archives (FIAF) organized a symposium on selection as part of the Karlovy-Vary Congress. The proceedings of that symposium, *Problems of Selection in Film Archives*, revealed that most moving image archivists were ambivalent on the subject. On the one hand most of the participants accepted the fact that archives must select in order to cope with the volume of material being produced at the time, at least with regard to nonfiction films. Very few archives in 1980 were willing to publicly admit that anything that could be construed as the *art* of the film should *not* be preserved. A survey conducted for the symposium revealed that many FIAF member archives had established a mechanism for appraisal and selection (thirteen members utilized advisory committees, fourteen members had internal regulations based on written criteria). There was only one volunteer to reply to the question, "Can you give us an example of a moving image or a type of moving image that you would either not select, or that is now in your archives that you feel should be deselected."[48] The only example was one offered by the film archives of the German Democratic Republic: the deselection of a short film on agricultural composting because it was a Bulgarian film that was already being conserved in Bulgaria!

There is no evidence that there is any greater consensus on selection or deselection among members of FIAF today. Severe financial constraints rather than shifts in policy have motivated film archives to deselect in recent years, particularly when dealing with formats such as nitrate stock film that demand a timely and significant investment in order to preserve the material. This does not imply that the deselected works should be destroyed! In almost every case there is now an archive somewhere in the world, possibly one with a specialized collection of moving images, that will accept it.

One of the most comprehensive and systematic reviews of the holdings and of their selection policies was conducted in the nineties by ScreenSound, National Screen and Sound Archive of Australia. As a result of their new selection policies they decided to repatriate dozens of nitrate prints to their countries of origin because they could no longer justify the investment in their long-term preservation and storage. Their policies will be discussed in chapter 4.

In fact all archives select, whether systematically, intuitively, or opportunistically, and while they compile lists of selections, they rarely compile lists of rejections. The reasons are obvious. To do so would be to risk alienating a producer or distributor whose goodwill is essential. Very few of the FIAF member archives enjoy the benefits of compulsory or mandatory legal deposit, and even those that do rely on the cooperation of the industry to implement the law. Another reason may well be recognition of the fact that a valid case can be made by someone for some purpose for the preservation of every frame of every moving image. Schellenberg, taking up Meisner's warning that "too great an abstraction is an evil," suggested that an imaginative archivist could find some reason for the retention of every document, thus reducing appraisal to the level of an intellectual game.[49]

The FIAF survey in 1980 revealed that relatively few archives have fully developed written guidelines to govern selection, and little has changed in the past twenty years. Even fewer archives had regulations for the rejection and formal disposal of rejected material in 1980. One such was the Films Archive of the Czechoslovak Film Institute operating under the general direction of the Managerial Board of the Czechoslovak Film. Under this system, which would appear to be ideal from a purely archival perspective, all national film productions were systematically monitored throughout their life cycle, and all production elements, whether negatives or prints, domestic or foreign, in all categories of production, were scheduled for retention for a period of years and then disposal at the end of that period, or for deposit with the Archives for long-term preservation.[50] This system ended with the dissolution of Czechoslovakia into the Czech Republic and Slovakia in 1993.

This was, of course, a comprehensive records management program, one that identifies all the elements relative to a given production and places them under control from the moment of manufacture (or importation from another country) to the point of disposal or deposit with the archives. In such a program, operating with the full cooperation of the producers and distributors, the principles of selection can be applied at every stage of the active life of the production to guarantee that the best possible material will be protected for archival purposes while avoiding the needless retention of large quantities of material that no longer serves any useful function.

Record scheduling at an early stage in the life cycle of records has become a standard feature of records management programs in many countries, and it is proving to be essential in the management of electronic records. The Association of Moving Image Archivists has recently established a Task Force on Digital Issues in order to explore ways to impose control on the increasing quantity of digital recordings that are a product of modern production methods in the feature film and animation film industries. Imposing archival control earlier in the life cycle of records may be the only effective way of coping with the enormous quantity of moving images currently being produced for both theatrical exhibition and television, and the U.S. national plan, *Redefining Film Preservation,* is based on the presumption that the major studios will implement such programs.[51]

This type of program is, of course, much more feasible in countries where production is a state enterprise and thus subject to central control. In the U.S., for example, despite the activities of several archives working in concert with the Library of Congress, the selection and conservation machinery was still inadequate to cope with the immense volume of production. The means of production are in the hands of thousands of independent organizations and there is no effective means of registration for well over half the estimated total annual production. In the U.S., as in all major moving image production countries, feature film and network television production represents only the tip of the iceberg in moving image production, and few archives in countries where there is no central control can afford the time, the money, and the storage space to do more than occasionally dip beneath the surface.

The rewards in appraising the total range of production when applying selection criteria used to be illustrated by the program of the National Film Archives in London (now the National Film and Television Archive). Working with four advisory selection committees (History, National Film Archives in London (now the National Film and Television Archive). Working with four advisory selection committees (His-

tory, Science, General [the film as art form], and Television) the Archives surveyed a very wide variety of sources that included feature
films, documentaries of all types, educational films, scientific and experimental film, and amateur film or *home movies,* whose informational
value with regard to location, association, period, or subject matter
made them worthwhile accessions. Because subject matter is as important as form in these selection criteria, the advisory committees include
subject specialists as well as historians, critics, and archivists.[52]

Unfortunately, the cost of operating such a system is considerable,
and when only a small proportion of the works selected can be acquired
in the absence of compulsory or mandatory deposit legislation (in the
fifties and sixties the London archives actually acquired less than 25
percent of the films it selected) it is difficult to justify. The committee
structure was abandoned in the seventies and replaced by staff selection, as is the practice with almost all other moving image archives.

Very few moving image archives actively review and reassess the
collection on a regular basis, and fewer still deselect on the basis of
current acquisition policy and selection criteria. The motivation to reassess past acquisitions increases when the condition of the holdings, or
a requirement to migrate to new formats, demands a substantial additional investment. Selection standards are rooted in the cultural and historical biases of the present, and if they change it is only logical that the
selections based on them should also be open to review. This also argues strongly for some mechanism to delay selection so that some sem-
blance of historic perspective can be achieved Since all moving images
have some informational value the criteria to be applied should incorporate some exclusionary factors that limit the selections. The History
Selection Committee of the National Film and Television Archive in
London adopted *A Guide to the Selection of Films for Historical Preservation* in August 1959 that excluded films whose subject matter
could be adequately dealt with in another medium. The test was actually "does the film record the subject matter better in this medium than
in any other?" and films whose loss, in the opinion of the committee
members, would not "be regretted," either for their subject matter or
their technique, by researchers several years later.[53]

This suggests that archivists should be prophets and, as been noted
by several appraisal theorists, one should be wary of prophecy as a
guide to selection. Nevertheless, moving image archivists must accept
that responsibility and, acting on the best advice available, make those
decisions. The alternative, given the volume of contemporary produc-

tions available, is either to fill the vaults with material of marginal value (*ephemera* in terms of content and form) until there is no storage capacity left for records of obvious value (based on form, content, or association), or to evade the issues entirely, as the national archives of the world succeeded in doing for half a century.

Although one can only applaud Herman Kahn's admonition that archivists should not act as cost accountants and allow a rigid cost/benefit analysis to determine what is preserved and what is destroyed, the question of costs cannot be ignored. Moving images arrive at the archives in a variety of formats, and in conditions ranging from excellent to so poor that unless immediate steps are taken to conserve the image by transfer, the information the record contains will be lost forever. Films on nitrocellulose stock are only one of the types of moving images that demand an immediate investment on the part of the archivist, if only for separate climate controlled vaults, if the films are to be preserved. Recent revelations about the fragile nature of acetate stock film and the *vinegar syndrome* show that even relatively recent films may demand urgent treatment. All substandard film for example, whether due to shrinkage or excessive wear must be transferred before it can be safely consulted for both internal processing or reference service. Almost all broadcast industry videotape formats will also have to be transferred before the records can be described and organized by the archives, and before any public access is possible.

The immediate archival investment can thus be considerable. The ongoing costs, in terms of environmentally controlled storage conditions and monitoring of the collections, the need to manufacture reference copies for every item in the collection if the originals are to be protected (the life of any film or videotape copy can be measured in the number of times it is viewed, and the number is not very large) and still permit public access, adds substantially to the costs. If cost is pressuring archivists in appraising paper records, it is an unavoidable and very substantive factor in appraising all media records, and often a determining factor in the final decisions on acquisitions. This should not be the case in an ideal world!

Although the genuine need for appraisal and selection standards is not expressed in the literature on moving images, most moving image archivists would probably recognize and would probably accept the basic principles on appraisal theory that have evolved in the writings on archives in the past century. In general these will serve both for non-governmental organizations that relate to moving images primarily as an art form, and to national archives whose orientation toward film is as an historic record.

The most basic of these, following Meisner, is that old age must be respected. Despite its comparative youth as a means of human communication (cinematography was demonstrated in most parts of the world by 1898), moving images have suffered so extensively from *benign neglect* by archivists and curators that all moving images produced before 1930 can be regarded as incunabula. In the United States, for example, only 15 percent of the estimated 4,000 feature films and 30,000 short films produced between 1910 and 1920 are known to have survived. For the twenties the figure is 25 percent. For American archivists, *triage* for the production prior to 1930 is a *fait accompli*, and there is no reason to believe that the survival rate in other countries is any higher. In fact there is every reason to believe that it is considerably lower, because American films were being distributed worldwide by 1920, while the productions of other countries were restricted to limited national distribution and, if the Canadian experience was typical, competed unsuccessfully for screen time with American films.

For countries in which the production and distribution mechanisms were devastated by wars and revolutions the date may, of course, be much later. For countries which have emerged from a colonial dependency, for example, all films produced in the territory by foreign filmmakers before independence may be of great value, regardless of content as influenced by the prevailing ideology. In countries in which moving image production is just beginning, all films produced in the country by foreign filmmakers may be of value for their location shots alone, or for their documentary record of places, people, dress, language, and customs which have changed radically during the upheavals of the twentieth century.

Where television began in the fifties and sixties, all broadcasts before 1970 should be acquired, as so much of what was broadcast live before 1960 has been lost, and so much of what was recorded on videotape in the sixties has been wiped.

Another principle relates to the concept of *documentary* value, as defined by Schellenberg and others, to the effect that records that do not testify to the history, organization, or function of the agency that generated them may still have informational value. Penelope Houston related the work of the appraiser at this stage to the work of the critic:

His job is to make up his mind about what the artist was trying to do,

then to consider how well he has done it. The third question is the
dangerous one: was it really worth doing in the first place? To ask it
implies that the critic is judging the work not on its own merits (that
favorite, elusive English phrase) but according to some system of
values, that, in fact, he has a theory.[54]

It is the archivist's task to determine if that value, in terms of meeting
the established needs of his or her contemporaries and the potential
needs of researchers in years to come, warrants the costs of acquisition
and processing *and* all the downstream costs in the years to come.

The archivist should be aware that moving images, intended as they
are for mass audiences, are part of the public record. In considering
their value as part of that record the normal tests of accuracy, objectivity, coherence, or fairness need not apply. To take an extreme example,
the faked news films that appeared following the outbreak of the Boer
War and the Spanish-American War are early attempts at the utilization
of film for blatantly propaganda purposes, and yet they remain significant documents on understanding that period *because they are fakes.*[55]

In a less obvious example, the documentaries produced during the
fifties designed to educate the general public on how to defend themselves against the atomic bomb are no longer regarded as either reliable
guides to survival or accurate accounts of the probable effects of nuclear warfare on a civilian population. The films are, however, a valuable record of government attempts to communicate directly with the
population on an issue that was, and remains, of paramount concern to
every person on this planet, and they accurately reflect the political
climate of the day and the ideologies of their sponsors.

The *science* incorporated in these films of the fifties, highly suspect
when examined from the perspective of a new millennium, brings into
focus the fact that the archivist cannot be expected to have the expertise
in every field necessary to evaluate the diverse documentation available
for selection, and that the appropriate expert should be consulted on
subject content and treatment. The final decision, which should not be
delegated, should remain with the archivist.

Applying theory to practice is difficult with the variety of challenges facing the moving image archivist. Given the sheer volume of
some genres of production such as serial drama from television, or
sports broadcasting that has reached the level of occupying whole
channels, or children's programs, or talk shows, or the vast output in
both traditional and computer-generated animation, just surveying the
output is exhausting. This is one of the reasons that some moving im-

age archives restrict their acquisitions from television to landmark productions or to films made for television, and why national plans for moving image preservation urge the broadcasters themselves to take responsibility for their own productions. The vast increase in the number of specialty channels only complicates the picture and the advent of digital broadcasting will make the task of archiving television, from both inside and outside the broadcasting organizations, even more challenging.

There are a host of issues that crop up in assessing moving images that may affect the final decisions, but in most cases should only alert the archivist to the responsibility he or she has in documenting the work so as to facilitate access. They include such issues as the authenticity of works purporting to be the results of ethnographic or anthropological expeditions; the reliability of *docudramas* in which real-life incidents have been dramatized; and the abuse of historic footage in compilation films.

Content and treatment are selection criteria for moving image archives that evolve naturally from the general principles governing appraisals by all archives, but there are three other appraisal principles that many nongovernmental archives apply that lie outside the normal appraisal policies of national archives.

The first of these, and the most difficult to deal with, is the complex question of aesthetics. Many private, nonprofit archives are devoted to the conservation of moving images exclusively as an art form, as an aspect of the national culture, whether the images are conceived in the country or flow in from abroad. They equate their collections with collections of paintings in the national galleries, and their prime criteria is whether the moving image selected advances the art by treatment of theme, or by technique, or by a combination of the two. Aesthetic factors tend to be highly subjective and aesthetic judgments are decidedly transitory. Iris Barry and her colleages at the Museum of Modern Art in New York were so selective on aesthetic grounds that they only accepted two of Buster Keaton's films when they were offered all of them, and they focused much more effort on German, French, and Russian films of the silent era than on those produced in Hollywood.[56] Such judgments are so transitory, in fact, that the strongest argument for a *nonevaluative* acquisition policy are the losses that occurred due to what has been perceived as the faulty judgment of the previous generation of archivists. The Langlois dictum that the archivist should not play God has been adopted as an operating principle to which some moving image archivists still adhere, although no national archives or library, including the Library of Congress, has been able to sustain the volume of intake that such a principle would entail if everything that was produced were deposited. If aesthetics is a factor, most archivists rely on advice from critics and theorists, and the results of competitions at film and television festivals.

The second principle, one that is peculiar to moving image archives, is the responsibility to document the history of the industry, or the evolution of its technology. Moving image archives attached to production organizations are very interested in firsts. The first sound film, the first color film, the first wide screen production, the first satellite broadcast, the first color broadcast, the first regional broadcast in an expanding network, are all milestones that such organizations should retain to document their own activities, and that archives should acquire to document the history of the industry.

For film archives milestones in the national production are very important, whether they represent technological change or trends in genres, break new ground in themes and treatment that press censorship limits, or establish new "stars", are all significant for such archives, although they may well meet other criteria set by national archives.

The third criterion that many nongovernmental moving image archives apply is an aspect of universal retention. In much the same manner that traditional archives designate certain record groups or series within groups (such as those relating to policy formulation) as of sufficient value to be retained in their entirety, some moving image archives designate certain producers or directors (occasionally writers, actors, cinematographers) as so significant in the development of the art and the industry that all their work should be acquired and conserved. In some cases this criterion may apply to a production entity (the work of the National Film Board in Canada is an example) although this practice tends to be restricted to production units that have had a limited history, or which have dominated a particular sector of the national production.

One approach to the appraisal of moving images that has generated some controversy has been an evaluation based on the sociological or psychological impact that moving images, especially fictional feature films, are presumed to have had on their audience. A pioneer in this field was Siegfried Kracauer, who identified the feature films produced in Germany in the twenties and thirties with the *national will* and the rise of Nazism.[57] Although much of Kracauer's work has been criticized as overstating the impact of moving images as opposed to the other economic, political, and social forces at work both inside and outside the country, recent studies have supported the view that feature films do reflect the currents and undercurrents at work in the society that produced them.

One example is the impact of the Cold War and the threat of nuclear war on American films of the fifties and sixties.[58] The problem for the archivist is that universal retention for feature films would appear to be the only solution if the needs of such researchers are to be met now and in the future, because neither the aesthetic quality of the productions nor the artistry of any of the cast or production crew is really a factor.[59] In fact, it is in the so-called 'B' pictures, the marginal productions on the fringes of the industry, that these characteristics of the national psyche can best be studied.

Research on feature films for their sociological or historic significance can concentrate on a single outstanding film (*Birth of a Nation, Le Regle de Jeu, Chapayev*) but the researcher increasingly wants access to as wide a range of the national production as is possible, both to place the outstanding productions in context, and because the so-called *program features*, the productions that conform to accepted formulas as to theme and execution, and which meet the needs of the production/distribution system, are less self-conscious, and thus more reflective of the national mood. This is another argument for universal retention, particularly as moving image critics writing now are no more likely to discern either the masterworks, or the works which indicate significant shifts in the direction of development, or to identify emerging talents, than the art critics who almost totally ignored impressionism were at the turn of the century.

To select among such productions is extremely difficult and, for the reasons stated, can result in serious errors in judgment. Most non-governmental moving image archives have adopted a policy of universal retention for feature films, at least for their national production, and for foreign films distributed in their country. The policy is sustainable only because, as compulsory or mandatory deposit is only operative in a handful of countries, the films they actually acquire are only a fraction of the total exhibited. At the very least, such archives would argue, all feature films should be retained for a number of years so that the selection can be made with the advantage of some historic perspective. Experience has indicated, however, that five years is not sufficient, and that at least a generation, or twenty years, is required to ensure that the judgments are firmly grounded.

Very few government archives have adopted this policy. The legal requirement of deposit in order to register for copyright has enabled the Library of Congress in the United States to build a very impressive collection of feature film productions, but even the Library does not expect to be totally comprehensive. One reason is that many independent, experimental, and pornographic films are never registered for copyright; another is that many films fail to achieve any commercial success and in the absence of a market the producers never complete registration by depositing a copy.

In many countries in which the archive is part of the state-controlled moving image enterprise, deposit of copies (and the original negatives after initial distribution) of all feature films is automatic. None of the organizations, however, are national archives. They function as part of the productions/distribution system, making copies of early films available to cine clubs, educational institutions, and for exploitation in secondary markets. In a few cases this includes documentary films, newsfilms, and television productions. In most countries, however, other governmental or nongovernmental archives have been given responsibility for actualities and television productions.

Fragmentation of effort and tentative steps to make up for years of neglect characterize the worldwide movement to conserve moving images as historic record and cultural artifact. In adopting the UNESCO Recommendation in 1980, the member states made a moral commitment to secure the resources necessary, but the volume of production still far outstrips the machinery necessary to appraise, let alone preserve, what is being produced. That this is a worldwide movement demanding cooperation and coordination among film and television archives, both governmental and nongovernmental, is becoming more and more apparent each year. One of the criteria for selection should be whether or not the copy in hand is unique or the best material to be preserved, at least as far as archival holdings are concerned. With the current volume of international distribution and exchange of moving images throughout the world, one of the prime tasks of the international federations and the regional organizations is to establish a data network between archives so that duplication of effort can be avoided, and so that the best surviving copy is permanently preserved.

There are many hazards inherent in a *one title/one archive* policy, and the experience of two world wars and innumerable national upheavals testifies to the losses that can occur; but with more and more archives finding it difficult to secure even minimal resources for the protection of the moving image heritage, surely some of the funds now being expended in preserving the critical or popular successes in every archives, as though it were the sole surviving copy, should be avoided.

Appraisal of moving images, as is the case with the appraisal of any type of documentation is far from an exact science; "it is at best an inexact science, perhaps more an art, and a conscientious appraiser, particularly an imaginative one with an awareness of research interests and trends, is apt to know nights of troubled soul searching."[60] In most archives it is not even an established procedure with a policy and selection standards or a detailed guide. Where appraisal procedures and practices have evolved from records management retention and disposal schedules these have largely ignored or bypassed moving images, concentrating on the disposition of broad record groups rather than the complexities of item-by-item selection. Few moving image archivists have been trained as archivists, in any case, so that the guidance in the archival literature and the theory, inadequate as it may be, is largely unknown to them. Among some film archivists there is still a great reluctance to destroy any moving image, arguing that if they cannot accommodate the volume, a worldwide network of archives should make it possible to conserve all moving images. All the international and regional associations recognize that while this should be a viable policy, and may be one some day, an intelligently applied appraisal policy is better in the short run than intuitive selections and chance that condemns many valuable moving images to destruction because no effort has been made to save them.

Notes

1. There are substantial bibliographies and overviews of current theory in Rick Klumpenhouwer, *Value Concepts in Archival Science*, unpublished Master of Archival Studies thesis, University of British Columbia, 1988; Jane Turner, *A Study of the Theory of Appraisal for Selection*, unpublished Master of Archival Studies thesis, University of British Columbia, 1992, Terry Cook, "Mind Over Matter: Towards a New Theory of Archival Appraisal," in *The Archival Imagination: Essays in Honour of Hugh A. Taylor*, Barbara L. Craig, ed. (Ottawa: Association of Canadian Archivists, 1992), 60-69; and Luciana Duranti "The Concept of Appraisal and Archival Theory," *American Archivist* 57 (spring 1994): 328-343.

2. Luciana Duranti, "The Concept of Appraisal and Archival Theory,"

American Archivist 57 (spring 1994): 329.

3. David Walden, "Stretching the Dollar: Monetary Appraisal of Manuscript," *Archivaria* 11 (1980/81): 101-7.

4. T. R. Schellenberg, "The Appraisal of Modern Public Records," in *A Modern Archives Reader: Basic Readings on Archival Theory and Practice,* Maygene F. Daniels and Timothy Walch, eds. (Washington, D.C.: National Archives and Records Administration, 1984) 68. Schellenberg's monograph on appraisal was originally published in 1956.

5. Gerald Ham, "The Archival Edge," in *A Modern Archives Reader: Basic Readings on Archival Theory and Practice,* Maygene F. Daniels and Timothy Walch, eds. (Washington, D.C.: National Archives and Records Administration, 1984) 326. Ham's article was originally published in 1975.

6. Margaret Hedstrom, "New Appraisal Techniques: The Effect of Theory on Practice," *Provenance* 7 (fall 1989): 1-21.

7. Terry Eastwood, "Towards a Social Theory of Appraisal," in *The Archival Imagination: Essays in Honour of Hugh A. Taylor,* Barbara L. Craig, ed. (Ottawa: Association of Canadian Archivists, (1992) 71.

8. Frank B. Evans, Donald Harrison and Edwin A. Thompson, comps. "A Basic Glossary for Archivists, Manuscript Curators and Records Managers," *American Archivist* 37 (spring 1974): 417.

9. UNESCO, *Final Report of the Expert Consultation on the Development of a Records and Archives Management Programme (RAMP) Within the Framework of the General Information Programme, 14-16 May, 1979* (Paris: UNESCO, 1979).

10. Brian Brothman, "Orders of Value: Probing the Theoretical Terms of Archival Practice," *Archivaria* 32 (summer 1991) 78-100.

11. Jane Turner, *A Study of the Theory of Appraisal for Selection,* (Master of Archival Studies Thesis, University of British Columbia, 1992) 7.

12. Cook, Terry, "Mind Over Matter" in *The Archival Imagination: Essays in Honour of Hugh A. Taylor,* Barbara L. Craig, ed. (Ottawa: Association of Canadian Archivists, 1992) 41.

13. Luciana Duranti traced this development in a six-part article: "Diplomatics," *Archivaria* 28 (summer 1989) 7-27; 29 (winter 1989-90) 4-17; 30 (summer 1990) 4-20; 31 (winter 1990-91) 10-25; 32 (summer 1991) 6-24; 33 (winter 1991-92) 6-24.

14. Theodore R. Schellenberg, *Modern Archives: Principles and Techniques* (Chicago: Society of American Archivists, 1956).

15. Hilary Jenkinson, *A Manual of Archives Administration* (Oxford: Clarendon Press, 1922).

16. Jenkinson, *Manual,* 11.

17. Luciana Duranti, "The Concept of Appraisal and Archival Theory4," *American Archivist* 57 (spring 1994): 334-35.

18. Public Record Office, *Guide to the Public Records, Part I, Introductory.* (London: Public Record Office, 1949).

19. Great Britain. Public Record Office, *Principles Governing the Elimination of Ephemeral or Unimportant Documents in Public or Private Archives* (London: Public Record Office. n.d.)

20. Schellenberg, *Modern Archives.*

21. Philip C. Brooks, "The Selection of Records for Preservation," *American Archivist* 3 (spring 1940): 221-34.

22. G. Philip Bauer, *The Appraisal of Current and Recent Records* National Archives Staff Information Circular, No.13 (Washington, D.C.: National Archives and Records Service, 1946).

23. Maynard J. Brichford, *Archives and Manuscripts: Appraisal and Accessions* (Chicago: Society of American Archivists, 1977).

24. Meyer H. Fishbein, "A Viewpoint on Appraisal of National Records," *American Archivist* 33 (Fall 1970): 175-87.

25. Harold T. Pinkett, "American Archival Theory: The State of the Art," *American Archivist* 44, (summer 1981): 217-22.

26. Brichford, *Archives and Manuscripts.*

27. Eastwood, "Social Theory of Appraisal," 76.

28. Hilary Jenkinson, Speech to the International Council on Archives, *Archivum* 1 (1951): 47.

29. Eastwood, "Social Theory of Appraisal," 89.

30. Schellenberg, *Modern Archives*, 13-16.

31. Hilary Jenkinson, "Modern Archives: Some Reflections on T. R. Schellenberg," *Journal of the Society of Archivists* 1 (April 1957): 148-49.

32. Andrew Raymond and James O'Toole, "Up from the Basement: Archives, History and Public Administration," *Georgia Archive* 6 (fall 1978) 26-27.

33. Felix Hull, "The Appraisal of Documents—Problems and Pitfalls," *Journal of the Society of Archivists* 6 (April 1980): 289.

34. Margaret Cross Norton, in *Norton on Archives: The Writings of Margaret Cross Norton on Archival and Records Management*, Thorton W. Mitchell, ed. (Carbondale: Southern Illinois University Press, 1975) 240.

35. Richard Cox, "The Documentation Strategy and Archival Appraisal Principles," *Archivaria* 38 (fall 1994): 15.

36. Brichford, *Archives and Manuscripts*, 2.

37. Ham, "Archival Edge," 328-29.

38. Eastwood, "Social Theory of Appraisal," 83.

39. Bauer, *Appraisal of Current and Recent Records*, 4.

40. Eastwood, "Social Theory of Appraisal," 83.

41. Frank Boles and Julia Marks Young, *Archival Appraisal* (New York: Neal-Schuman, 1991) 101.

42. Boles and Young, *Archival Appraisal*, 103.

43. Helen Samuels and Richard C. Cox, "The Documentation Strategy and Archival Appraisal Principles: A Different Perspective." *Archivaria* 38 (fall 1994): 11-36.

44. Yves Pérotin and R. Maiquant, "Les documents audio-visuels." in *Manuel d'archivistique* (Paris: S.E.V.P.E.N, 1970) 540-62.

45. Among the many commentators on this aspect of mass communications are Erik Barnouw, *The Sponsor: Notes on a Modern Potentate* (New York: Oxford University Press, 1978); Neil Postman, *Amusing Ourselves to Death: Public Discourse in the Age of Show Business* (New York: Penguin Books, 1985); Jerry Mander, *Four Arguments for the Elimination of Television* (New York: Morrow Quill Paperbacks, 1978).

46. International Federation of Film Archives (FIAF), *A Handbook for Film Archives* (Brussels: FIAF, 1980).

47. International Federation of Television Archives (FIAT), Recommended Standards and Procedures for Selection and Preservation of Television Programme Material. (London: FIAT, 1996).

48. International Federation of Film Archives (FIAF), *Problems of Selection in Film Archives* (Brussels: FIAF, 1980).

49. Schellenberg, *Appraisal of Modern Public Records*, 62.

50. Vladimir Opela, "Problems of Selection of Film Materials and Archival System in Czechoslovakia," in *Problems of Selection in Film Archives* (Brussels: International Federation of Film Archives, 1980) 9-23.

51. *Redefining Film Preservation, A National Plan: Recommendations of the Librarian of Congress in Consultation with the National Film Preservation Board* (Washington, D.C.: Library of Congress, 1994).

52. Clyde Jeavons, "Selection in the National Film Archives of Great Britain." in *Problems of Selection in Film Archives,* (Brussels: International Federation of Film Archives, 1980) 25-51.

53. National Film Archive, *Guide to the Selection of Films for Historical Preservation* (London: British Film Institute, 1959).

54. Penelope Houston, *Keepers of the Frame: The Film Archives,* (London: British Film Institute, 1994) 129.

55. Raymond Fielding, *The American Newsreel, 1911-1967.* (Norman: University of Oklahoma, 1972. There have been a number of studies on film and propaganda that document reenactments and the deliberate misrepresentation of moving images: Nicholas Pronay and D. W. Spring, *Propaganda, Politics and Film, 1918-45,* (London: Macmillan, 1982); Gary Evans, *John Grierson and the National Film Board: The Politics of Wartime Propaganda* (Toronto: University of Toronto Press, 1984); Bruce Cummings, *War and Television,* (London: Verso, 1992).

56. Haidee Wasson, "The Cinematic Subtext of the Modern Museum: Alfred H. Barr and MoMA's Film Archives." *The Moving Image* 1 (spring 2001) 1-28

57. Siegfried Kracauer, *From Caligari to Hitler: A Psychological History of the German Film,* (Princeton: Princeton University Press, 1947).

58. Jack Shaheen, ed. *Nuclear War Films* (Carbondale, Il.: Southern Illinois Univesity Press, 1978); Nora Sayre, *Running Time: Films in the Cold War*

(New York: Doubleday, 1982).

59. There have been a number of studies pursuing Kracauer's ideas and investigating the relationship between feature films, historic understanding and national identity: *Past Imperfect: History According to the Movies*, Mark C. Carnes, ed. (New York: Henry Holt, 1995); Barbara Deming, *Running Away From Myself: A Dream Portrait of America from the Films of the Forties* (New York: Grossman, 1969); Jeffrey Richards, *Visions of Yesterday* (London: Routledge & Kegan Paul, 1973).

60. Leonard Rapport, "No Grandfather Clause: Reappraising Accessioned Records," *American Archivist* 44 (spring 1981): 149.

Chapter 3

Form and Function of Moving Images

Whether produced by government agencies, by private organizations, or by individuals utilizing the medium as a means of artistic expression or personal documentation, moving images can still be categorized by provenance, function, and form. None of these categories is exclusive, of course; provenance can define function, function can dictate form, and form can limit function.

If few moving image archives have the opportunity to apply the archival maxim *respect des fonds,* all moving image archivists should recognize the fact that no document is produced in a vacuum and thus the textual documents associated with the production of a moving image may be as significant as the moving image itself. Completed films or television broadcasts may carry credits that tell the archivist and the researcher who made the images, and even where and when, but they rarely tell how, and most important, why. Incomplete and/or unedited production footage seldom reveals anything inherent to source or purpose.

Form is used here in a different sense than in traditional archival theory. The form of a textual document is an essential element in assessing its trustworthiness, its authenticity.[1] The form of a moving image relates to its structure and its intended purpose: fiction versus nonfiction, factual versus impressionistic, live-action versus animation (or a fusion of the two), instructional versus propaganda (if a valid distinction can be made between the two!), etc. Form in this sense should not be confused with *genre,* the attempt to categorize moving images, particularly fiction films, as types such as *westerns, horror, comedies, drama, film noirs, science fiction,* etc., with many subcategories within each major category.

Function

There are three aspects to provenance and moving images. The first is the identity of a document as part of a series or group. Television productions are frequently broadcast as series, and individual episodes lose part of their archival value if they are totally divorced from the series and from the related documentation on the production and on the impact of the series. The archivist cannot assume that in fifty years the researcher will recognize an episode from *Dallas* or *Friends* or *Coronation Street*, regardless of how popular they were at one time. Series episodes should always be appraised in the context of the series, and whether all the episodes are retained, only specimens, or the entire series is rejected, the decision should be based on an evaluation of the entire series.

In the past documentary films were also produced in series—*The March of Time, Canada At War, Why We Fight*—and the same concern for provenance should apply. Whenever possible the entire series should be appraised along with all related documentation, as the whole may be considerably more valuable than the sum of the parts, particularly in light of the production organizations' or sponsors' objectives considered in the context of the social, political, or economic issues of the day.

Related documentation in the form of textual records present all archives, governmental and nongovernmental, with problems in maintaining the integrity of the series or records group. By their nature moving images demand special storage facilities and handling so that the images will be physically separated from related text and must be linked through inventory or catalog descriptions. The damage caused by this separation is intensified in national archives that elect to process nontextual materials by media in separate departments or divisions.[2]

If the production entity is a government agency, the production files and administrative records will probably also be accessioned. If there is no common inventory or catalog, the researcher who fails to make the appropriate inquiries may miss significant materials in the other media.

This second aspect of provenance—the symbiotic relationship of the images and the documentation that explains how and why they were made and how they were used—is equally important with regard to the work of individuals whose moving images documented their lives as a complement to the correspondence and diaries that may make up their papers. Here, too, the images should be appraised in the context of the total collection, although the images may have informational value that warrants their retention even if the rest of the collection is rejected.

A third aspect of provenance for the moving image archivist stems from the relationship of the work being appraised to the entire corpus of the image-maker or production organization. This may be of greater concern to a nongovernmental moving image archive with the documentation of the career of a particular individual or a production unit as one of its objectives. However, any archives appraising moving images as part of the national cultural heritage should evaluate individual items on offer in the context of the total output of a director, producer, or studio. If the decision has been made to select all of the productions associated with a personality or production organization, identification of the item under review with the individual or entity will be all the justification that is needed.

Knowing why a moving image was produced, and how successfully it reached its intended audience and achieved its objective, can be a very important element in the appraisal process. If the purpose was primarily commercial and the venture was not a success, the moving image will not have functioned effectively as part of the public record. If there are no artistic factors arguing for its retention, and nothing about the circumstances of its production to warrant special attention, there is a prima facie case for rejection.

However, commercial failure alone should not constitute grounds for rejection. The artistic factors associated with an ambitious failure, or a critical success whose innovative techniques were "ahead of its time," may be sufficient to justify retention. In some cases the "failure" may be due to circumstances surrounding the production and distribution of that work that documents the history and development of the medium in that country, and in those cases, especially if related documentation is available, the evidentiary value for researchers interested in the structure and operation of the moving image industry may well warrant retention.

Where function is overtly associated with a political ideology or a commitment to societal change, this may prove to be a determining factor in appraisal. If the moving image is designed to inform or persuade an audience as part of a deliberate campaign that involves other forms of communication, the rules of provenance dictate that the images should be retained as part of the total public record. If they stand alone they may still illustrate the intent or the policies of the sponsoring agencies in a manner that is not possible with conventional textual records.

The documentaries and news films which the National Socialists in Germany produced to propagate their political and social philosophies before and during World War II are very well known, but there are many examples of films and television programs that have influenced public opinion and had a significant impact on national policy even though most of them were not produced under state control or direction. The United States' involvement in Vietnam, for example has been described as the first "television war," and there is no doubt that it will be difficult to comprehend the shift in American public opinion and the changes in American foreign policy without reference to the images that brought the battle zone into the living rooms of millions of Americans.[3] Those images, as much as the record of debates in the Congress, the miles of government records, and the library shelves full of reports and books, are all part of the public record and should be conserved.

Many moving images have a highly specific function, and it is very unwise to attempt to appraise them without assessing the entire record created by that activity. The use of moving images as a research tool, for example, may result in high speed, or slow motion, or infrared, or photogrammetric, or microphotographic film studies associated with scientific experiments that are incomprehensible without support documentation. They may be of immense value in documenting scientific discovery, or relatively worthless records of phenomena that can easily be recorded at any time. The same is true of moving image studies of animals in the wild, and nature studies of all kinds that exploit the cinematic marvels of time-lapse, or the camera's ability to endure extremes of heat or cold for long periods and to record whatever occurs in front of the taking lens. Archivists must rely on the advice of experts in assessing records such as these, and much will depend on how the moving images relate to other records already in the archives or available to the archives to further document the activity. Careful consideration should be given to the uniqueness of the moving images and whether the information they contain is captured elsewhere in the record in a more readily accessible form. Given the cost of conservation and storage over the long term, and the miles of test film that can result, the archivist should be convinced that the informational and/or historic value over the long term justifies the expenditure.

Form

Beyond the basic questions of whether the moving images under re-view are or pretend to be fact or fiction, an archival appraisal should also consider the image-makers' method, the form in which the con-tents are presented. This can vary from a straightforward didactic exploration of a stated theme, a kind of "living textbook," to com-pletely free-form expressionism, a sequence of images, connected perhaps only in the image makers' subconscious, that are designed to evoke visceral responses, if they evoke any at all.

In the documentary alone in recent years, experiments in form and method have introduced *cinéma verité* or *direct cinema,* dramatized documentaries or *docudramas,* and the *open inquiry,* in which the im-age-makers' experiences in capturing the images and in manipulating them are as much a part of the content—commenting on the action, ex-plaining what was shot (and not shot) and why—as the reality outside the editing room that the image-maker set out to explore. In extreme cases content (and structure) that proves to be intractable may be sacri-ficed to form and the result is a work that may not meet criteria as a documentary record nor justify preservation for technique alone.

The myth of absolute objectivity that was supposed to be the docu-mentarian's goal at all times, has not stood up well under rigorous analysis in recent years. We are now much more aware of the subjectiv-ity inherent in the choice of camera position, lighting, and music, as well as in the choice of subjects to be interviewed and in the portions of those interviews that will be edited in or out. The myth persists because some documentary filmmakers, borrowing a phrase from Jean-Luc Go-dard, who was referring to the cinema he and his colleagues were trying to create in the sixties, still maintain that "film is truth at 24 frames per second."

In the early days of television when most documentaries were being produced by, or purchased by, the news or public affairs departments, producers tended to dictate a form in which opposing points of view are carefully balanced. This *on-the-one-hand and on-the-other-hand* struc-ture is still the standard form for documentaries, and they can normally only be assessed at one level—the uniqueness of the information con-veyed and the importance of the personalities interviewed.

The form is most restrictive in formula fare made for popular entertainment. Television 'soap operas' and most situation comedies, for example, are produced to such a rigid formula that one or two specimens can serve as examples for a year's production. Most dramas (crime, romance) produced in series fall into this category, as the demands of the form seldom allow the writers or producers the luxury of experiments with character, language, or theme. Archivists concerned with the role of the director as the chief creative component in filmmaking may be interested in *formula* productions by a director whose oeuvre has been selected for preservation just because the form is so restrictive. It is, of course, sometimes a challenge to distinguish one episode of a series from the others by identifying the individual style of an *auteur*.

When considering form, the basic principles of age and quantity can help guide selection practice. If the item in hand is the sole survivor of an extensive series it would of course, be appraised differently than if a hundred were available for selection. If the item is very old, in moving image terms (prior to 1950 for film, prior to 1960 for television), and only ten of the hundred original productions have survived, the archives may decide to retain all of them, or at least attempt to place the episodes not required with other archives.

Notes

1. Luciana Duranti, "The Concept of Appraisal and Archival Theory." *American Archivist* 57, (spring 1994): 328-45. For a much more elaborate description of form and issues of authenticity and reliability in textual archives see Duranti's six-part article, 'Diplomatics', in *Archivaria* 28-33, 1989-1992.

2. For a thorough airing of the pros and cons on this issue see the exchanges between Terry Cook, "The Tyranny of the Medium." *Achivaria* 9 (winter 1979-1980): 141-49 and Andrew Birrell, "The Tyranny of Tradition." *Archivaria* 10 (summer 1980): 249-52. The middle ground was presented by Ernest Dick et al, "Total Archives Come Apart." *Archivaria* 11 (winter 1980-1981): 224-27.

3. Michael J. Arlen, *Living-Room War*. New York: Viking, 1969.

Chapter 4

Appraisal Policies and Practices

Applying theory to practice is always a challenge. With no consensus on policies and standards, each archives is forced to adopt its own approach to appraisal, and for many there is no articulated methodology in place. For some nongovernmental archivists focusing on feature films there is no need for policies and standards: they have a list of films they want for their archives, based on their knowledge of contemporary production and drawn from the established canon of great works embodied in the literature and the only problem is securing access to them.

For moving image archivists with a broader mandate there needs to be some direction on appraisal and selection or the collection will simply grow, by chance, opportunity, or accident, without any real reference to the universe of images available. Because conditions vary so greatly from country to country with regard to legal factors (the presence or absence of copyright or mandatory deposit, restraints imposed on producers licensed by the state), fiscal factors, the relationship of the archives to the production sources, etc., there is no one model that will serve all archives. Hopefully there are some ideas in the programs and policies outlined here that will prove useful.

UNESCO

A good departure point for a discussion of appraisal policies in relation to moving images is *Recommendation for the Safeguarding and Preservation of Moving Images,* a document adopted by the General Conference of UNESCO in October 1980. It was the result of a great deal of discussion with archivists in the International Federation of Film Archives and the International Council on Archives and represented a consensus of their views as modified to meet somewhat strenuous objections from the film industry. The *Recommendation* was based on three premises.

The first was that moving images, *all* moving images, are "an expression of the cultural identity of peoples . . . and form an integral part of a nation's cultural heritage, as well as constituting important and often unique testimonies, of a new dimension, to the history, way of life and culture of people."[1]

The second was that the establishment of an officially recognized archives, or a network of officially recognized archives, would be required to safeguard and preserve "any part or all" of the national production. The legal and administrative measures to accomplish this objective could include "voluntary arrangements with the holders of rights for the deposit of moving images, acquisition of rights by purchase or donation, or the institution of mandatory deposit systems through appropriate legislation or administrative measures." [2]

The *Recommendation* did not consider *copyright deposit*, legislation that requires the deposit of moving image works in order to register for copyright, because the United States was the only country in the world with that requirement, and the practice was contrary to international conventions on copyright then in force. *Mandatory deposit*, usually associated with archives or library legislation, is the legal requirement that the producer or distributor deposit a copy of the work with a designated institution (there may be more than one institution named). The deposit may be at the cost of the producer/distributor or at the cost of the designated institution. In Canada, for example, the National Archives Act of 1986 gives the Archives the right to purchase, at the laboratory cost of reproduction, a copy of any moving image work produced or distributed in Canada.

The third premise was that "the safeguarding of all moving images of national production should be regarded as the highest objective." Until such time as the technology made this feasible, however, archives could "establish principles for determining which images should be recorded and/or deposited for posterity, including 'ephemeral recordings' having an exceptional documentary character." A high priority should be accorded all moving images whose "educational, cultural, artistic, scientific, and historical value" form part of the nation's cultural heritage. Selection, when necessary, should be based on the "broadest possible consensus of informed opinion," should take particular account of the "appraisal criteria established by the archival profession," and should only take place after "sufficient time has elapsed to allow for the necessary perspective."[3]

Indicative of the uphill struggle to achieve recognition of the value of moving images is that the resolution is a *recommendation* rather than a *convention* that would have obligated member states to ratify and implement its terms. The *Recommendation* was in many ways a compromise that reflected the realities of the tenuous relationship existing between archives and moving images. Rather than use "national archives," for example, to describe the organizations to be charged with the task, the term "officially recognized archives" was adopted so that private, nonprofit organizations or other state agencies that had been given or had assumed responsibility for the conservation of moving images in the public interest could be included. The *Recommendation* also suggested that a network of officially recognized archives' could be established to achieve the objectives, with each, perhaps, specializing in one type of record, either by form or by source.

Again, although the *Recommendation* proposed total retention for all moving images in the national production as the ideal objective, it recognized that this might not be feasible economically and suggested selection criteria "be based on the broadest possible consensus of informed opinion and should take particular account of the appraisal criteria established by the archival profession."[4] Compliance of the producers or distributors could be either voluntary or mandatory, and it was left to national legislation to determine exactly when and how the deposit would be made, and to specify the physical nature of the material to be deposited.

At the time the *Recommendation* was adopted there was not one organization, governmental or nongovernmental, that was achieving the ideal objective: the safeguarding of every moving image of the national production. The situation in most countries fell into one of four categories:

❑ No organization, or program, responsible for the safeguarding of moving images;

❑ A limited program, highly selective, by an organization that may have been "officially recognized," but was probably not a state institution;

❑ A mix of governmental and nongovernmental organizations, with the governmental organization restricting its acquisitions to government record moving images (produced by or sponsored by government departments and agencies) and the nongovernmental organization, probably affiliated with a film or television production organization or an educational institution, restricting its accessions to the production of the affiliated production organization or to production from the private sector—films as document or art;

❑   A division of responsibilities between two or three gov-
    ernmental archives, especially where moving image pro-
    duction is a state monopoly, with film records in one,
    television records in another, and, perhaps a further divi-
    sion between actualities (news film and documentaries)
    and fiction film.

Too many countries fell into the first category, a situation that the
International Federation of Film Archives (FIAF), the International
Federation of Television Archives (FIAT) and the International Council
on Archives, the three international organizations active in the field in
1980, armed with the *Recommendation,* hoped to change in the years
ahead.

With the introduction of television services in countries where
there had been little or no previous film production, the safeguarding of
those moving images became a stimulus toward the establishment of
organizations, or programs within existing organizations, to protect
these resources. Unfortunately, new television services have generally
been careless about protecting their own production resources. The records accumulate as long as space is available, if the videotape is not
erased and recycled, and large blocks of the holdings are eliminated,
often without further examination, when space is no longer available.

Ironically, television organizations learn the value of properly organized production libraries or archives—the terms are used interchangeably by television organizations—when anniversaries occur and
the desire to celebrate their own history motivates a review of their
holdings. In fact, the reuse of production resources cannot only enrich
current productions, but in reducing the quantity of new material
needed to fill the program schedule it can effect savings that, if properly managed, can totally offset the cost of the library or archives.
Footage from past productions can also be sold to outside producers for
additional revenue. In recent years the international marketing of production resources has become such a lucrative business that many television organizations have established separate divisions or even separate companies to handle the trade.

Even when the television organization has put in place a program
to protect the archival resources, there is still a problem in balancing
the obligations that the archives has to the organization and its function
as a conservator of part of the national cultural heritage. How the public

gains access to those resources, and who should pay for the service are issues to be resolved, either through secondary distribution arrangements, or through the deposit of reference copies with organizations equipped to provide this service.

If the selection standards are to reflect *further use* obligations—the Canadian Broadcasting Corporation's distribution program operated through the National Film Board of Canada in the mid-eighties was called the *Further Use Program*—they may have to be modified so that both objectives can be met. In fact, the intelligent application of a well-developed appraisal policy by a television production organization, or a well-established film production organization, will result in selections for permanent retention that should closely parallel those of an archives established solely to safeguard moving images in the public interest.

Public broadcasters such as the Canadian Broadcasting Corporation (CBC) and the American Public Broadcasting System (PBS) have attempted to develop appraisal policies that meet these dual objectives, but in both cases they have been unable to secure sufficient resources to fully implement the policies. While a well-managed conservation program (whether called an archives, a library, or just a production resource) may generate sufficient revenue through sales of footage to outside producers to offset the running costs of the program, they cannot be expected to cover the cost of providing public access. In the case of the CBC, the situation has been further complicated by the effort to integrate the collecting mandate of the National Archives of Canada and its holdings of thousands of hours of broadcasts—both film (kinescope) copies and off-air tape recordings—with the archive program of the network.[5]

From an operational television production perspective, these dual objectives are sometimes perceived as being in conflict. It has taken more than twenty years for a workable compromise to evolve in the United Kingdom between the National Film and Television Archive (NFTA, now part of bfi Collections of the British Film Institute), the British Broadcasting Corporation (BBC), and the independent production companies regulated by the Independent Broadcasting Authority (IBA). The Copyright Act of 1988 gave the NFTA, and three other designated institutions, the right to record programs off air for archival purposes. The Broadcasting Act of 1990 required the IBA companies to provide direct financial support to the NFTA to record their programs off air and the NFTA is designated as their official archives. The BBC maintains its own archives, although it also deposits copies of certain broadcasts with the NFTA on request of the NFTA, and under the terms of the Broadcasting Act underwrites the cost of reference service at the NFTA. The NFTA applies it own selection criteria and records the broadcasts, some 7,000 a year, directly off air.

In recent years, as both the NFTA and the BBC have refined their selection criteria, there has been general agreement on what should be preserved. The difference lies in the quantity and type of material (primarily news film) that the BBC decides to retain to meet its own future production requirements, or for its program sales.

In order to ensure that everything that should be retained is retained, the BBC has instituted a two-stage selection program. A very broad selection is held in the production *library,* and after several years a further selection is made as additions to the *archive,* where use of the original materials is strictly controlled.[6]

Based on the history of archives that are members of FIAF, in countries in which there is not yet an organization that is systematically safeguarding moving images, the activity in film conservation will probably grow out of exhibition programs in cinematheques and university media study programs, or through government agencies assuming responsibility for government record film and then broadening their selection standards.

The cinematheques and university study programs normally begin by acquiring projection prints of feature films that are regarded as international *classics,* and then add both feature films and documentaries from the national production. These *collections* are not actually functioning as *archives,* however, until their administrators can begin to protect their projection prints with master material—original or duplicate negatives or intermediate printing elements—and provide secure storage facilities.

At this stage these organizations may select only those titles that are currently required for the exhibition program or to meet the immediate demand for film study. The selection standards, if any are articulated, may stress aesthetic factors, potential research use, and documenting the industry. For such organizations to function effectively as national film archives all films of the national production would have to be systematically appraised so that selections are based on long-term values rather than short-term needs and special interests.

In restricting accessions only to government-produced or government-sponsored films, a government archives may be carrying out its primary responsibility toward government records, but it will not, of course, be functioning effectively as a national moving image archives in the meaning of the *Recommendation.* Such an archives could, how-

ever, perform its primary limited function and still act as one component of a network of archives which, when acting in concert, can
achieve the objectives of the *Recommendation.*

What follows does not pretend to be a worldwide survey of moving image archives, and does not pretend to be a comprehensive review
of activities in the countries mentioned. The countries and archives featured have been selected to illustrate the ways in which structures have
developed to identify and conserve elements that constitute the moving
image heritage, and to illustrate the implementation of appraisal policies.

FIAT

The International Federation of Film Archives first adopted *Recommended Standards and Procedures of Selection and Preservation of
Television Programme Material* in the eighties, and issued a revised
edition in 1996. The *Standards* begin with the premise that "in an ideal
world, all material created for television would be preserved to the
highest possible technical standards and properly documented." In a
less than ideal world, where there are financial, operational, and technical restraints, appraisal policies and selection standards are essential.
The aim is to apply a consistent policy "to ensure that no material of
potential value is discarded" and to select for both operational and cultural purposes. The danger is that the decisions to discard will be implemented by persons not qualified to assess the informational value of
the material, and, moreover, by persons acting under the pressure of
short-term expediency. These pressures are greatest during the early
years of the life of a television production organization, state owned or
private, and such organizations are urged to establish and implement
policies selection standards as soon as possible to avoid the mistakes
and the losses suffered by most television organizations that began
broadcasting in the early fifties.

The FIAT *Standards* warn of the impact that technological innova-
tions, such as the introduction of videotape recording in the early sixties, can have on retention policy when the pressure to erase videotapes
for reuse in the broadcast cycle led to the loss of many important programs. It is ironic that just as more motion pictures from the 1896-1912
period survived as paper prints in the Library of Congress through the
accident of copyright law than survived in the vaults of the producers,
so more kinescope recordings (16mm film records of live television
broadcasts in the fifties) survived than did videotape recordings in the

sixties, because so many videotapes were recycled in the production process.

In the last forty years we have seen black-and-white television replaced almost entirely by color television, diminishing the value of the black-and-white videotape recordings to the production organizations (especially low-band recordings), the introduction of 1-inch helical format videotape for broadcast purposes in 1965 to replace the 2-inch quadruplex format that was the standard in the industry since 1956, and we are now witnessing the transition to various competitive and noncompatible digital formats. One commentator has remarked that if the rate of change in the technology of television broadcasting continues, by 2010 they will be changing the format in the middle of a broadcast! There is no standard in sight, and archivists are debating the viability of developing a magnetic storage medium designed specifically for long-term conservation. Unfortunately there is no general agreement on the viability of such a project, let alone on the technology to be adopted or adapted for the purpose. Work is underway as I write on defining the specifications of a long-term storage medium and on methodology for adding *tombstone* data (basic facts on the origin of the recording and on its manufacture) to every recording.

The additional challenge to archivists is the need to reassess the videotape collection each time a transfer to a new format is required to avoid obsolescence, because of the very substantial costs involved. Even if the decision is to transfer everything there will be the need to identify priorities if the transfer is a multiyear project.

The FIAT *Standards* also consider the authority for selection, and recommend that responsibility for determining policy be shared with production departments, sales departments, and technical departments within the production organization, and with an advisory committee representing educational, cultural, and critical interests in the community. This consultation could range from consideration of general policy and development of selection criteria to a review of retention schedules and decisions on individual broadcasts. The final decision should, however, remain with the archivist, a position endorsed by all archival manuals.

On the timing of selections, the FIAT *Standards* recommend that all actuality material be retained for a minimum of five years *before the initial evaluation*, to give the selectors sufficient perspective with which to perform effectively. For fictional material this period is reduced to two years. A reassessment is recommended after a further five years, after ten years, and then every decade to determine if the selections warrant long-term retention.

Another aspect of timing, and one that concerns archivists of all moving images, is that all the broadcasts and the production elements available for selection should be protected immediately after initial transmission, and that the *original* materials (whether negatives of films, or master videos) be deposited in the archives. Costs may force the archives to accept lower standard deposits (1/2-inch videocassettes, for example, in place of 1-inch videotape, or Digital Betacam in place of the original digital recording), but the objective must be to acquire and conserve the best possible quality as close as possible to the date of the first transmission. This issue has become much more complicated with the introduction of digital recording technologies, and what constitutes original materials is moot in a production environment where transfers can be effected with no loss of image or audio content

The FIAT *Standards* also provides a list of suggested selection criteria that is designed to meet both the needs of the production organization and the larger community. The list developed in 1981 was modified in 1996 with descriptions of typical broadcast output assigned to one or more of seven categories. The categories, in order of priority, are:

A.   Actuality material of historic interest in all fields;
B.   Actuality material as a record of a place, an object, or a natural phenomenon;
C.   Interview material of historic importance;
D.   Interview material indicative of opinions or attitudes of the time;
E.   Fictional and entertainment material of artistic interest;
F.   Fictional and entertainment material illustrative of social history;
G.   Any material, including commercial and presentational, illustrative of the development of televisual practices and techniques.

The *Standards* recommend that both transmitted and untransmitted material be selected from all *genres* but that transmitted material, part of the public record, should be given a higher priority. For some genres, such as news, news analysis and comment, current affairs, and documentaries, the recommendation is that *all* transmission tapes be selected, as well as the unedited material that is judged of value for further broadcast purposes. Topical magazines and discussion programs, on the other hand, are considered to be more ephemeral, and if they cannot all be selected, the recommendation is that priority should be given to programs covering subjects that have had a particularly significant effect on society. Where cost is a very restrictive factor, at least representative examples of such programming should be retained.

The recommendation is that all event broadcasts be retained, as transmitted, for their historic and sociological value, and all drama, music, and art performances for their cultural value. For general entertainment programs—talk/chat shows, variety shows, comedy, stand-up, one-man shows, situation comedy, popular music shows or concerts—the suggestion is that the archives may be more selective but aware that if only examples are retained every show should be reviewed to determine if some feature—the guests, the performer, a special occasion, a technological innovation, etc.—warrants its selection. Game shows and quizzes may be considered as ephemeral but here again, examples should be selected as reflective of the popular culture that responded to them.

The FIAT *Standards* were essentially developed for active broadcasters concerned primarily with potential reuse of a corporate asset, and with almost every genre, or type of program, a nonprofit or state archive would approach selection differently. One example is the recommendation that *all* children's programs and *all* educational programs be retained. There is no rationale for this decision in the document, although the potential for retransmitting such programs and their use as a resource for new forms of hypermedia and interactive programming may be a factor, but it is unlikely that a national archive would decide to preserve that quantity of essentially repetitive broadcasts in the long-term. The same would probably be true of the recommendation on sports programs, although even the broadcasters recognize that some selection will be necessary given the sheer volume of such broadcasts.

Of interest in the *Standards* is the concern that *presentation* elements—the order in which the programs are presented, the station breaks, the program promotional spots, the logos, the commercials, etc.—also be preserved. The only effective way to do this is to record an entire day of transmissions at least once a year.

United States

In the United States, the National Archives and Records Administration (NARA) has maintained custody over government record film to a greater or lesser degree since that institution was established in 1934.

In the years following World War II this activity was greatly expanded in order to cope with the vast quantity of news film and documentaries produced in support of the war effort, as well as the audiovisual productions of what had become a very substantial government image-making activity.[7]

At the same time, NARA broadened its acquisition policy to include all moving images (from television as well as from private films producers) that related to the history of the United States. With the donation of the Ford Film Collection of news film and documentaries in the fifties, this was interpreted to include all newsreels produced in the United States. With the acquisition of the entire Universal newsreel collection, a gift that included the copyright so that the archives could make them freely accessible for any use, NARA became one of the most important resources for documentary footage in the country.

What constituted a *historic* film was difficult to define precisely as it included filmed biographies of prominent political or military leaders even though the films were made in Hollywood and featured the stars of the day. By acquiring these, NARA widened the area of overlap with the moving image accessions of the Library of Congress (LC) as evidence of registration of copyright.

As sketched in the chapter on history and organization, the mechanism for effecting a comprehensive collection of motion pictures at LC existed at the time cinematography was first presented to an audience in 1895. In order to complete registration for copyright, producers were required to deposit a copy of the work, but as motion pictures were not included in the copyright act until 1912, they deposited the films as a series of photographs, which were covered under the existing legislation, printed out on long strips of paper. These paper prints, some 3,000 in number, were the beginning of the LC collection. Under the change in copyright legislation in 1912, producers were permitted to deposit copies of the films themselves, but the Library did not have the resources to house them, and only a very small fraction of the films copyrighted between 1912 and 1946 entered the collection.

Not all images produced and distributed in the United States however, are registered for copyright (television programs that will not receive secondary distribution are excluded for example) and of those that are selected, not all of them are acquired by the Library. The estimate is 70 percent.[8] As is the case with many national libraries and legal deposit, LC can elect to register without accepting custody of the moving image itself. Given the immense volume of productions presented to the Library for registration, the percentage rejected is significant.

The reasons for rejection are repetition, as in the case of television series or productions for instructional or educational purposes; subject matter, such as pornographic films, where only specimens are selected; or volume as in the case of commercials, where only examples taken from each year's production are acquired.

The network of archives that constitutes the *national* moving image archive in the United States is complex and now includes special collections at other government agencies (such as ethnographic and anthropologic film at the Smithsonian Institute and aerospace film at the National Aeronautics and Space Agency) as well as significant collections at private, nonprofit organizations such as the Museum of Modern Art Film Department (feature films, documentaries, art films, and video art), the Film Department at George Eastman House (feature film, documentaries), the Film and Television Archives at the University of California (feature films and all aspects of television broadcasting), the Museum of Broadcasting (exclusively radio and television broadcasts), the Vanderbilt Newsfilm Archives (exclusively network television news broadcasts), and others devoted to commercials, political campaign advertisements, industrial and sponsored films, horror and fantasy films, etc.[9] Those that are members of the International Federation of Film Archives meet annually to discuss issues of mutual interest and to ensure that duplication of effort is held to a minimum. Many of the smaller archives collaborate through the programs and projects of the Association of Moving Image Archivists.

In addition, each of the major television networks in the United States and the major specialty channels maintains its own archives, with the news and public affairs department maintaining a separate archives to meet the immediate needs of production. For the nongovernmental moving image archives in the United States, selection of both domestic and foreign moving images is either on the basis of content (highly specific in some cases and demanding expert consultation) or the significance of the production in the history of the art and the industry. These are essentially the same criteria as all cinematheques with general collections employ, and they relate to creative collaboration (the individuals or creative units whose work the archives has selected for comprehensive documentation); representation from identified periods of production, regional production, or any "school" of production; genre formation and development (as these allow critics and archivists to categorize productions and to simplify comparisons and quality judgements); milestone production in relation to form, content, technology, or to the economics of production and distribution; and critical and/or popular successes that become part of the public record or part of the common culture and thus part of the national heritage.

The histories of the moving image collections at the Museum of Modern Art (MoMA) and at George Eastman House (GEH) are linked to the lives and personalities of Iris Barry at MoMA[10] and James Card at GEH.[11] In both cases the approach to acquisition was decidedly based on aesthetics. Card began as a private collector, and after his collection was institutionalised at GEH, the selection standards he applied stemmed from his own sense of what constituted "the art of the film." Iris Barry, who was the driving force behind the establishment of the Film Department at MoMA in the thirties, had equally strong ideas on what constituted the great works of the cinema, works that would be worthy of a place in the Museum among all the other great works of twentieth century art.

In their own way they illustrated the limitations (as well as the strengths, it should be added!) of collection building based on the knowledge and taste of a single individual, and the fact that we are rooted in the cultural biases of our own time.

Czech Republic

The situation in the former Czechoslovakia has changed dramatically since break-up of the country into the Czech Republic and the Slovak-Republic. The system in place was one that most closely approximated the objectives of the UNESCO *Recommendation.* In contrast to the substantial network of organizations that are engaged in moving image conservation in the United States, there were only three organizations involved in Czechoslovakia, and they were all regulated by the State Archive Administration and the Central State Archive. In accordance with legislation passed in 1974 in the Czech Socialist Republic and in 1975 in the Slovak Socialist Republic, the Film Archive of the Czechoslovak Film Institute was confirmed as responsible for the conservation of the Czech film production (the activity had been established after the Second World War and the principles of selection had been introduced as early as 1969), the Slovak Film Archive had the mandate for Slovak film production and a Czechoslovak Television Archive was to retain all of the productions from that medium that met the criteria for selection.[12]

As articulated by the Film Archive of the Czechoslovak Film Institute the appraisal policies were based on the works of Czechoslovak archival theorists—in particular Jaroslav Vobata and Tomas Fiala—as interpreted and codified by a working group attached to the State Archives Administration. The document this group developed, *Definition of the Scientific Principles of the Selection of Film/Audio-Visual Records,* provided specific policies in relation to Czech film production. In essence these are very similar to those usually adopted by cinematheques with general collections—aesthetic judgments as to "quality," representation of periods of filmmaking, reflection of social or political character of an epoch or an historic event, creative collaborators, genre development, innovation and experiment, award winners, technological milestones, etc.

What was strikingly different in the application of these criteria in Czechoslovakia is the method employed both to select acquisitions and to dispose of the films that have not met the criteria. All film productions in the country were under the surveillance of the Czechoslovak Film Commission for the Discarding of Film Materials, and no films could be "discarded" without the authorization of the Commission. All the major production, distribution, and laboratory organizations were represented on the Commission with the representative of the film archive acting as Chair. It should be noted that the Commission did not select acquisitions for the archives; the archives retains that responsibility. The Commission, however, controlled the disposition of the moving images while they were still in the hands of the producers, distributors and laboratories.

In effect, all film productions in Czechoslovakia were subject to a records management program in which they were all scheduled for either eventual deposit with the archives or disposal. With the totality of the production registered and protected, the Film Archive of the Czechoslovak Film Institute then worked with two commissions to effect selection: one identified older productions, documented them, and evaluated them as potential acquisitions; the other, evaluated and selected contemporary productions. Both commissions utilized the same criteria, although factors such as uniqueness, scarcity, technological milestones, and simple age obviously played a more decisive role in evaluating older productions. One by-product of the systematic review of all surviving productions was the repatriation of unique prints and/or master material for foreign productions that did not meet the selection criteria.

The Czechoslovak system, imposing centralized management and uniform selection standards, drastically reduced the damage caused by splitting the moving image heritage resources among three archives. Researchers would still have to visit three organizations, but there was little duplication of effort and little chance of important material slipping through the net.

Since the fall of the Communist regime and the break-up of Czechoslovakia, the archive, which had been struggling for autonomy under the Czech Film Institute, succeeded, in 1992, in achieving independence as the National Archive of the Czech Republic. Although funding for the Czech archive has been secured to continue the preservation program, the privatisation of the film and television industries and the lack of a legal deposit mechanism has crippled the acquisition program and eliminated the application of central appraisal and selection policies.[13]

Australia

ScreenSound, the National Film and Sound Archive of Australia, is one of the few archives that has decided to review its appraisal policies and selection standards, *and* to apply the new standards to a complete re-assessment of the collection. They based the review on a document they drafted in 1998, *Collection Development Policy: Collection Development Guidelines and Selection Matrix.* This laid out an acquisition policy that focused primarily on the national production, formulated the key collecting principles, described the types of material to be acquired in twenty-four sectors—actuality, advertisements, current affairs, documentary, features, home movies, etc.—evaluated the present strengths and weaknesses of the collection in each sector, and outlined the principles on which material now in the collection would be deselected.

The selection matrix grid is designed to facilitate assessing material from any of the twenty-four sectors against seventeen descriptors. A documentary, for example, might relate to social change; diversity and history; cultural change, diversity, and history; a significant historic event; innovation in style or technology; or all of these. If the work in question meets the revised collecting mandate as stated in the principles and also scores high in the matrix, it is probably a suitable candidate for selection, assuming the physical condition is acceptable and the archive does not already hold a dozen prints of the same work.

The same approach is applied when surveying the existing collection and, if material fails to meet the new standards for selection, it is deselected. The focus on the national production, for example, caused the Archive to remove and repatriate to their country of origin dozens of nitrate prints of foreign films that did not meet the criteria for retention and whose continued preservation would have cost significant funds that the Archive preferred to allocate to higher priority holdings.

The descriptions of the collecting priorities for each sector are detailed enough to act as a manual for junior staff (the whole policy document is 69 pages). The priorities for advertisements, for example, list:

- ❑ Industry award winners
- ❑ Examples of innovative production
- ❑ Examples of socially significant campaigns (for example, the 1994 Victorian drunk-driving campaign)
- ❑ Examples of controversial campaigns (for example, the naked-man-must-be-gay advertisement, AIDS awareness)
- ❑ Advertisements that have become part of the Australia's collective memory or resulted in words or phrases becoming part of the vernacular

The priorities for home movies include the following:

- ❑ The home recordings of both high profile and ordinary Australians
- ❑ Material which illustrates Australia's indigenous and cultural diversity, or otherwise provides an alternative perspective to what is currently held in the collection
- ❑ Material which consolidates collections from specific regions and eras

ScreenSound's objective is to create a national collection that is representative of all facets of Australian life, in all regions. Their collection policy recognizes, however, that it will not be possible for them to be comprehensive, even for the national production, and that they are part of a network of custodial institutions that collectively should ensure that the Australian moving image heritage will be preserved.

Russian Federation

Dividing the responsibility for appraising and safeguarding the national production among two or more archives without centralized management may lead to some duplication of effort (not always a bad thing, as it ensures that very important documents are completely protected) and overlapping of functions. In the old U.S.S.R., for example, the state film archive, Gosfilmofond, was established in 1948 to conserve all fiction films made for theatrical distribution. This was accomplished by a system of legal deposit and was designed to be comprehensive for all films in this category. Other films—commercials advertising films, films sponsored by government departments and other state organizations, documentaries of any length—were deposited in the Central State Archive of Film, Photographs, and Documentation at Krasnagorsk. Television productions were conserved in the separate archive maintained by the state television production organization. Again, three organizations to consult if the researcher wishes to exhaust all the possibilities for moving image documentation on a given personality or subject.[14]

In the case of the U.S.S.R. there were also three sets of selection standards. Gosfilmofond, focused on film as part of the cultural heritage—including foreign films circulating in the country—and adopted criteria based on aesthetics and cultural significance, although in practise they attempted to acquire the totality of the national feature film production, even if access to copies of films that were judged politically unacceptable had to be restricted. Krasnagorsk focused on film as historical record and attempted to be comprehensive for all news film and documentaries, again with restricted access to material that had been censored or withdrawn from circulation. The state television production archive applied selection criteria designed to establish a production resource that would meet the future needs of broadcasters. The potential for duplication is obvious as documentaries, particularly feature length documentaries on central issues of the day, cannot be excluded as part of the cultural heritage, and, in fact, Gosfilmofond selected certain major documentaries for retention in that collection even though the title may have been conserved at Krasnagorsk. Again, films initially produced for television or later transmitted by television, both fiction and nonfiction, that may also be conserved by the television archives.

The break-up of the old Union of Soviet Socialist Republics in recent years has led to the creation of film archives in many of the now independent republics, some autonomous and some attached to state archives or to other cultural institutions. Like moving image archives everywhere, they are all struggling to find the funds to preserve and service the works now in their care and to acquire the works they have identified as culturally and historically important. In many cases, they are attempting to repatriate master material or prints that they consider to be part of their national production from the archives in the Russian Federation.

Notably absent from moving image conservation in the Czech Republic and the Russian Federation, and indeed throughout most of the world, is any role for the central state archives. Apart from a regulatory or administrative role, practical implementation of moving image selection and conservation policies has been delegated, or in some cases simply abandoned, to one or more organizations, state supported or privately funded.

Argentina

The situation in Argentina is somewhat atypical of Latin America in relation to government action, but typical, unfortunately, in relation to results. Following the Second World War the Archive General de la Naçion, the national archives, recognized the need for a program in which moving image records produced in the country would be systematically appraised, selected, and conserved. An archive of motion pictures, photographic records, and sound recordings was established, and legislation was enacted to require the deposit of documentary films and news films. Feature films, television, and radio were, however, excluded from the deposit requirement, and very few early films were acquired.[15]

In the absence of government action on feature films a private foundation, Fundaçion Cinemateca Argentina, was established to acquire and conserve what had survived of the moving image heritage from the nitrate era, pre-1950. With a severe loss (unfortunately typical of countries in Latin America)—of the 550 feature films known to have been produced in the silent period (prior to 1930) only a handful, less than 50, have been located and conserved—there is no question of selection for the pre-1950 productions: everything that has survived is valuable either for its intrinsic merit, or as a rare example of production in the period.[16]

Government legislation to protect contemporary film production in the sixties unfortunately failed to appreciate the difference between a study collection and an archives. All feature films of the national production were to be deposited as a single copy in the National Institute of Cinematography. These copies, used for student reference, will inevitably be worn out, if not damaged, through use. A program for protecting and conserving contemporary production is obviously an urgent need, but developing appraisal policies in the absence of a practical program to acquire the films is a hollow exercise. The national archive has not yet committed the resources necessary to establish an effective program in this area. The private archive, Fundaçion Cinemateca Argentina, was concentrating its limited resources on the productions of the nitrate era, as these were in the greatest danger. Unfortunately, a disastrous fire a few years ago, in facilities that were completely inadequate for nitrate storage, severely damaged the program. Only a limited number of current film productions are really being conserved for the long term. Television productions are being held by the production organizations for their own future needs, and are thus subject to the economic pressures of broadcasting, which can range from destruction of archival resources to save costs on storage to mergers, in which entire production libraries are eliminated as unnecessary overhead.

The situation in Argentina is typical of the conditions to be found in practically every country in the world prior to 1960, and of the situation in more than half the countries in the world today. This is particularly true of the countries in Africa and Southeast Asia, where moving image production was either historically under the control of colonial authorities, the result of production by foreign visitors, or nonexistent prior to independence.

With the emergence of strong, central archives for all government records, the need to safeguard the oral and visual records of the national cultural heritage is being recognized as a high priority. For countries with a rich oral tradition, sound recording collections have already been established in many state archives, and one of the significant criterion for the selection of moving images is its value in the documentation of folklore, customs, traditional crafts, and language in societies experiencing rapid change. Where such records were produced in the past by visitors and exist in foreign archives, there is a growing desire to repatriate them under bilateral agreements as suggested in the UNESCO *Recommendation*. There are financial and legal obstacles to overcome, but there is little doubt that this will be a key objective for moving image archives in the region. It is one of the issues that regional groupings like the Southeast Asia-Pacific Audiovisual Archives Association are now discussing.

Again, in countries where functional literacy is still far from universal, the media of films and television has become an essential tool in communicating with the electorate and in propagating government policies in every aspect of life. Central state archives are recognizing the need to acquire and conserve these both for their evidentiary value in documenting the activities of government departments and agencies, and for their information value in documenting people, places, events.

Malaysia

The development of a moving image conservation program in the National Archives of Malaysia is typical of the situation in many countries in the region. The highest priority is given to government sponsored nonfiction production in film and television. If there is selection from television, the archives tend to concentrate on nonfiction films made for television rather than entertainment or general interest programs. Although there is growing awareness of the sociological and cultural value of fiction feature films and popular television programs, such as serial domestic drama, these are not generally regarded as high priorities. Once again the cost of conservation and the volume of production act as a deterrent, and there is a tendency to rely on the major production organizations in film and television, both governmental and nongovernmental, to safeguard their own productions until the central archives are funded and equipped to assume the responsibility.[17]

The National Film Department was established in 1946 and holds some 30,000 cans of film in its archive; Radio and Television Malaysia began in 1963 and has transferred most of its film holdings to videotape while it has moved through changing technology—2-inch quadruplex to 1-inch helical to Betacam SP—in production and in its archive. The National Library Deposit of Library Material Act of 1986 mandated that each production organization should "make, keep, and preserve a master copy of all its productions as a "back-up copy," and to "provide for safe-keeping and preservation a release copy of its production to the National Archive and the National Library."[18] In addition the National Archives was to seek out and recover, if possible, copies of works made in Malaysia or dealing with Malaysia that are held in other countries.

The problem with that decision is that neither the Archives nor the Library can provide a reference service with a single copy of the work that is supposed to be held for "safe-keeping and preservation." At a minimum they would have to hold two copies of the work, and then request additional copies from the masters held by the production organizations when the reference copies are worn out or damaged. In general, the ability of a production organization to balance out its obligations to the long-term preservation of the material in its archive and its obligations to the ongoing production program has always been in doubt. Even with the current recognition that corporate archives are a valuable asset, and not an administrative overhead, there have been too many examples of corporate actions that have endangered the archive or crippled its ability to function to argue that this is a viable long-term solution to the conservation of a vital component of the national cultural heritage.

Canada

Reliance on major production organizations, governmental and nongovernmental, to act responsibly in the protection and long-term preservation of their own productions was, in effect, the policy of the National Archives of Canada (NAC) for the first seventy-five years of cinematographic activity, and for the first twenty years of television broadcasting. Unfortunately, none of the governmental moving image producers were mandated or funded to safeguard their productions, and the nongovernmental producers reacted to the exigencies of the marketplace. If the material could be exploited commercially, it was retained and protected. If it could not, and there were costs associated with retention, it was frequently destroyed, or in the case of nitrate film it was allowed to self-destruct.[19]

When NAC first established a division to acquire and conserve moving images in the early seventies, the objective was to coordinate and expand an existing conservation project on recorded sound (oral history and radio broadcasting) and a project in identifying and locating surviving films from the nitrate era, pre-1950. In the process, a nongovernmental moving image conservation program (the Canadian Film Archive of the Canadian Film Institute) was absorbed and in due course the National Film, Television and Sound Archives (NFTSA) emerged to assume responsibility for safeguarding all government moving image records and to establish a comprehensive national collection of moving images and recorded sound.[20]

The issue of whether or not to integrate moving image and recorded sound services in central archives is not a simple one to resolve.
In the Canadian situation the archives had already established a photography division, as well as divisions in pictures, maps, and machine-
readable records. If these nontextual media were being introduced into
the archives today it is doubtful whether a strict divisional separation
by media would be adopted. Arguments for and against integration
tend to revolve around *respect des fonds*: government files containing a
variety of media must be physically separated (although every effort is
made to preserve the intellectual integrity of the file by cross listing
and/or cross indexing the contents), or researcher convenience and effi-
ciency on access (obviously with divisional separation by media, the
researcher will have to move from division to division to ensure that he
has examined all the relevant documentation), or communal requirements for technical services and storage conditions. These factors were
considered in the decision to integrate moving images and recorded
sound at NAC, but to a large extent the decision was based on common
sources (the Canadian Broadcasting Corporation was by far the single
largest source for both radio and television broadcasting) and common
appraisal criteria.[21]

One of the key questions to ask of any media document proposed
as an accession for a national archive is whether or not the information
it contains is available in any other format of documentation. If the answer is positive there may still be valid intrinsic reasons for retaining
the moving image, but if there are no valid reasons, the item in hand is
a candidate for disposal. In considering the integration of moving images and recorded sound, this question was extremely important as
practically all events in Canadian public affairs (press conferences, political party conventions, elections, debates in Parliament, commission
hearings) are now normally documented by sound recordings and moving images. If the moving images capture both the sound and the images there is obviously no need to retain the sound recording. Conversely if the sound recording contains most of the information
provided by the moving images perhaps only the sound recording, relatively inexpensive to accession, store, and conserve, need be retained.

A similar relationship between photographs and moving images
needs to be explored. Does the motion add significantly to the information conveyed, or will a photograph function as well? Again, if the answer is positive, the relative costs of conserving a photograph, or even
a file of photographs, as opposed to the costs associated with the con-

servation and long-term storage of a single reel of film can constitute a strong argument for retaining the photographs and discarding the film.

The situation in Canada also involved establishing a national program of moving image conservation that recognized the need to conserve and service production by language and by regional origin. The Cinémathèque Québécoise in Montreal had been in existence for several years prior to the serious involvement of the national archives in moving image conservation and continues to carry out its special responsibilities for French language film productions although the acquisition program of the national archives is bilingual and comprehensive, if not exhaustive, for Canadian feature films and documentaries.

In addition, the national archives had been encouraging and promoting the development of moving image conservation programs in provincial archives and regional museums for documentation of regional interest. This has become particularly important with regard to television production, where the quantity of production on a regional basis is well beyond the capacity of the national archives, and in any case would not meet the selection criteria that is rooted in a concept of *national* historic significance.

Even if NAC could absorb this documentation, the argument that such records should remain in the regions where they can service regional research remains, and counters the argument that the researcher, present or in the future, will be better served by centralizing all documentation of any value. Given its history, in a country the geographic size of Canada, regionalism is a fact with which all national cultural agencies must contend. The existence of a coordinated network of regional archives will inevitably modify the appraisal policies and selection standards of NAC. Intelligently interpreted and applied, the results should be a more effective and efficient moving image conservation program.

Germany

An excellent example of federal government coordination of moving image preservation, in relation to film at least, can be seen in the Federal Republic of Germany. Not only has the national program consolidated the physical custody of the surviving film heritage, centred on the Bundesarchiv, or national archives, but the acquisition policies of the three major film archives have been integrated to eliminate duplication and to ensure that as broad as possible a spectrum of productions will be appraised and safeguarded.

Following the World War II that witnessed the dissolution of the Reichsfilmarchiv—the archives the National Socialists established in the thirties and attached to the state controlled film industry—a national archives for the Federal Republic was established in Koblenz. By 1954 the Filmarchiv, a division of the Bundesarchiv, was given responsibility for securing and safeguarding prints of government film productions and of government-sponsored or funded feature and documentary films.

About the same time the German Democratic Republic established the Staatliches Filmarchiv (national film archive), and one of its chief tasks was to secure and safeguard the pre-1945 films from the Reichsfilmarchiv that were being repatriated by the U.S.S.R. One of the chief tasks of the Bundesarchiv was to receive and conserve the films confiscated from production organizations in Germany by the U.S. at the end of World War II, and which were gradually being repatriated to the Federal Republic. In time as well, the Bundesarchiv, like the National Archives and Records Administration in Washington, began widening its selection policy to embrace films that documented political, social, cultural, economic, or scientific developments in the Federal Republic.   As an extension of the government record film acquisition policy this could be literally interpreted to justify practically any film of the national production.[22]

In the sixties, the activities of the Bundesarchiv were supplemented by the formation of two private organizations that later became state institutions supported at the local level.   The first was the Stiftung Deutsche Kinemathek, which was closely associated with the Academy of Film and Television in Berlin.   The prime objective of the Kinemathek is to conserve and document the feature films of the national collection and to build an international collection to support film study and educational distribution.

The second, the Deutsche Institut for Filmkunde, was actually initiated as a private collection and was institutionalised in Wiesbaden in the late fifties.   Working in association with official regulatory bodies and agencies in the German film industry, the Institut is primarily concerned with documentation on the domestic and foreign production, the safeguarding of documentary films, and nontheatrical distribution.

The potential for duplication of effort and overlap in functions was apparent for over twenty years, but as cultural matters were the prerogative of the states it was not until 1978 that an agreement between the federal authorities and the state of Berlin could be concluded.   The agreement established a "Cinematheque Association" (Kinemathekverbund) embracing the Bundesarchiv, the Kinemathek and the Institut, under which the Bundesarchiv would be given the responsibility of storing all of the master material of the other organizations, restoring and conserving the films to the highest possible standards, and making reference copies available to the Kinemathek and the Institut as required for their exhibition, distribution, and film study activities.

With the reunification of Germany, the Bundesarchiv took over responsibility for the collection of the East German archive, the Staatliches Filmarchiv, the federal program was extended to all of Germany. The Cinematheque Association ensures the application of a coordinated appraisal policy so that no films of value are lost and there is no duplication of effort. The criteria remains as broadly stated by the federal archives, with each of the state archives enriching the selections from their particular perspective: films as art and culture, both domestic and foreign, by the Kinemathek in Berlin; and films as informational and educational documents by the Institut in Wiesbaden. Although the Cinematheque Association Agreement allows for the inclusion of other organizations, there are still a number of film acquisition and conservation programs operating independently (one for film in science and education in Munchen-Grunwald, one for scientific film in Gottingen, and the Munich Filmmuseum which specializes in the conservation and restoration of the early German feature film), and there is no reference to the archives of television. Each of the private networks in the Federal Republic has its own production archives, although they are coordinated to some respect in their appraisal policies and retention schedules. By utilizing common processing procedures they function as one large resource for the networks they serve, but there is only limited public access, and the overlap with the work of the Bundesarchiv with relation to films made for television and films subsequently transmitted by television is apparent. Given the very heavy involvement of the networks in the Federal Republic in the co-production of films and in film financing (both fiction and nonfiction) in recent years, a common phenomena in every country in which these two activities are not controlled by a single agency, this overlap in archival activities can only prove a disservice to the researcher and an inefficient use of usually scarce resources.

Appraisal guidelines for moving images, where they exist, are never very specific. At best they consist of terminology that is open to interpretation. The National Archives Act of Canada empowers the archives to acquire works that are of "national historic significance," a phrase that has been used to justify the acquisition of all types of moving images, as well as a very wide range of other material, textual and nontextual. Legislation in other countries refers to documents that are of "cultural value" or of "social importance" without any attempt to define what those terms mean. Attributions of value will vary from institution to institution and from archivist to archivist, even when relying on the same set of general principles. This is not necessarily a bad thing, given what we know about generational and cultural bias, but it does make it difficult to establish an acquisition policy that can be defended as objective and reflective of the entire society the archives serves.

Notes

1. UNESCO, *Recommendation for the Safeguarding and Preservation of Moving Images*: Adopted by the General Conference, Belgrade, 27 October 1980, (Paris: UNESCO, 1981) 3.

2. UNESCO, *Recommendation*, 5.

3. UNESCO, *Recommendation*, 5-6.

4. UNESCO, *Recommendation*, 6.

5. For an informative discussion of this issue see Thomas Connors, "Appraising Public Television Programs: Towards an Interpretive and Comparative Evaluation Model." *American Archivist* 63 (spring/summer 2000): 152-74; Ernest J. Dick, "An Archival Acquisition Strategy for the Broadcast Records of the Canadian Broadcasting Corporation." *Historical Journal of Film, Radio and Television* 11 (1991): 253-68; and Greg Eamon and Rosemary Bergeron, "Selection Factors for Audio-Visual Archives." Appendix B. *Fading Away: Strategic Options to Ensure the Protection of and Access to Our Audio-Visual Memory.* Ottawa: National Archives of Canada, 1995.

6. British Broadcasting Corporation, *Report of the Advisory Committee on Archives,* (London: BBC, 1979).

7. William Murphy, "The National Archives and the Historian's Use of Film," *History Teacher* 6 (1972): 119-54.

8. Larry Karr, "The American Situation," in *Problems of Selection in Film Archives,* (Paris: International Federation of Film Archives, 1982): 55-78.

9. For an informative account of the moving image preservation movement in the United States at the end of the twentieth century see Sarah Ziebell Mann, *American Moving Image Preservation, 1967-1987* (M.A. Thesis, University of Texas at Austin, August 2002).

10. Haidee Wasson, "The Cinematic Subtext of the Modern Museum: Alfred H. Barr and MoMA's Film Archive," *The Moving Image* 1 (spring 2001): 1-28.

11. Jan-Christopher Horak, "The Dreamer: Remembering James Card." *The Moving Image* 1 (spring 2001): 203-210.

12. Vladimir Opela, "Problems of Selection of Film Materials and the Ar-

chival System in Czechoslovakia." in *Problems of Selection in Film Archives* (Paris: International Federation of Film Archives, 1982) 9-25.

13. Vladimir Opela, "What Future for Film Archiving in Eastern Europe? The Case of the Czech Republic." *FIAF Bulletin* 46 (April 1993): 3.

14. Mark Strotchkov, " Final Remarks," in *Problems of Selection in Film Archives* (Paris: International Federation of Film Archives, 1982) 105-7.

15. Wilhelm Khote, "Archives of Motion Pictures, Photographic Records and Sound Recordings," (Paris: International Council on Archives, 1972).

16. Cosme Alves-Netto, et al, "Latin America," in *Problems of Selection in Film Archives* (Paris: International Federation of Film Archives, 1982) 5-8.

17. Sam Kula, "Audiovisual Documentation in Archives," *Southeast Asian Archives* (Special Issue1983) 3-6.

18. Habibah Zon Yahya, "Preserving Television Transmissions: Strategies for Acquisition, Appraisal, Storage and Use," in *International Council on Archives, Proceedings of the 13th International Congress on Archives, Beijing, 2-7 September 1996,* (Paris: International Council on Archives, 1996) 310-316.

19. Sam Kula, "Conserving the Canadian Image," *Journal of the University Film Association,* 27 (1975): 55-57.

20. Doug Herrick, "Toward a National Film Collection," *Film Library Quarterly* 15 (1980): 5-25.

21. Sam Kula, "Archiving television." *ASCRT Bulletin,* 17 (1982): 5-11.

22. Friedrick Kahlenberg, "Toward a Vital Film Culture: Film Archives in Germany," *Quarterly Review of Film Studies* 5 (1980): 255-261.

Chapter 5

Related Documentation

Appraisal policy should include documentation that is generated both during production (production files, legal and financial records, correspondence, scripts, posters, stills) and after the production has reached its audience (press books, interviews, reviews, critical articles). This assessment, should, of course, consider ancillary documentation (memoranda, correspondence) relating to the entire production program (or the series, if an episode is being assessed), other forms of communication that may have been generated for public information at the same time, and corporate or government policies that relate to the moving images in hand.

Appraisal of such documentation frequently occurs at two levels. If the moving image exists and has been accessioned, the documentation should add to what is known about the circumstances of production and the public reaction to the work; facts, in other words, that are not discernable from examining the moving image. The material should be distinctive if not unique, and descriptive; where it is repetitive and bulky, consideration should be given to selecting only specimens, particularly of publicity materials, while maintaining the integrity of the file.

If the moving image is not known to exist, or has not yet been conserved in the public interest, the related documentation may be the only means of learning about the work, of gaining an impression of the production. In these cases the assessment should be more generous so that the researcher has as much material as possible in order to imagine the work, to reconstruct it mentally, and, when necessary, the archivist has as much guidance as possible in reconstructing it physically.

Documentation generated during the course of the production can include the following:

Production Files. Obviously files should only be retained for production selected for retention, unless the entire series is being retained as a record of production activities. Such files may contain finding aids, shot lists, continuities, assignment reports, contracts, disposition of rights, etc., that can be invaluable in processing the production and in providing physical and intellectual access to the material. They can provide insight as to the intent of the image-makers, why certain choices were made, and on the constraints placed on the image-makers by economic and political forces beyond their control.

Production files may relate to, or may be part of agency or corporate administrative files that provide context for the production program. The aims and objectives of the sponsoring agency, whether an industrial corporation, a government department, a nonprofit charitable organization, a trade or professional association, or a religious group, will help establish the purpose of the productions and possibly position the productions as part of larger campaigns to effect social change. This may directly affect the assessment of their archival value.

Scripts. Care should be taken to distinguish between preliminary studies (treatments), drafts, shooting scripts, and cutting copies (scripts which conform exactly to the film as finally edited). An examination of all three in sequence may reveal more of the creative development of the concept than any one of the three. Shooting scripts that include directors' or producers' handwritten notes, deletions, corrections, are obviously of the greatest value, but any autographed or marked script may of value even though the production itself may be marginal.

Set Designs and Costume Designs. These may range from simple sketches to very elaborate drawings, and as they have become highly collectible they have increased in value. In some cases they represent aspiration rather than execution, and they are even more valuable for illustrating that gap. The artists involved in set designs may have achieved reputations in other forms of art that make their designs valuable regardless of whether the film or video production itself has value.

Animation. The documentation associated with animation productions may consist of key artwork, storyboards (outlining the action and indicating dialog, and all the character drawings (usually on cellulose acetate, and hence known as *cels*) and background drawings that are necessary to create an animated film. These can be tremendously voluminous—a half hour of animated film may require between 12,000 and 15.000 drawings!—and the challenge is to determine what portion of the material has archival value. Selecting this kind of material has been complicated by the substantial market for cels, normally marketed when mounted with backgrounds taken from the film, that has developed in recent years.

Stills. These may be categorized as (1) scenes from the production taken to publicize the work at the time of production, although not all such shots actually appear in the final edited version; (2) frame enlargements made from the production itself; and (3) production stills showing the process of production. Again, all stills have a much greater value if the production itself is not known to exist. If the production does exist, production stills will probably be of greater value, as they illustrate process and they may capture other creative collaborators, such as directors, producers, and cinematographers, who are not as frequently photographed as the leading players. Stills have had a very well defined market for many years, and comparable market values should allow a reliable assessment.

Posters, Press Books, Advertisements, Programs, and Trailers. Public perception of a moving image production is conditioned to a great extent by the manner in which the production is presented, the publicity campaign. If that reaction is to be understood, the materials that prompted it (especially when associated with the *trailers*, or previews of coming attractions, made to promote the film) should be conserved. If the production is not known to exist, this documentation may also be a valuable source of information on the creative collaborators that produced the work and on the nature of the work itself. In recent years the trailers have become miniproductions in their own right, often incorporating more skill and creative imagination than the film itself.

Film posters have been marketed by galleries and offered at auction since almost the beginning of cinematography. They have been associated with some of the great names in twentieth century art and rare original posters from the silent era regularly sell for thousands of dollars. At their best they encapsulate the essence of the film and the key selling points from the producer's perspective.

The archival and dollar value of press books and programs vary enormously and depend almost entirely on the reputation of the films themselves. The assessment also varies with how elaborate the press book or program is, and how many photographs it contains. Autographs and/or connections with personalities in the film will, of course, also affect value.

Models and Props. Many archives will direct three-dimensional objects to museums if they are perceived to have value. Many others will happily add such objects to their collections if they are associated

with recognized masterworks. The *collectibles* market in movie memorabilia, and extending to television series as well, now includes almost
anything associated with the productions in the way of models and
props, and the staggering prices achieved by props such as *Rosebud*, the
child's sled from *Citizen Kane* or Dorothy's slippers worn in the *Wiz-
ard of Oz* has focused attention on their monetary value if not their archival value.

Newspaper and Periodical Clippings. These contain critical reviews, interviews, and publicity about the production. They can provide
background information that is not apparent from a viewing of the film
itself. In dealing with documentaries, for example, it may of great importance to know when certain sequences were shot, exactly where they
were shot, and who was actually behind the camera at the time. The
reuse of earlier footage from other productions, for example, may be
identified and revealed in such interviews, or the arrangements that
may have been necessary to substitute footage shot elsewhere for footage that was not obtainable at the location. The whole issue of the authenticity of the work may be in question, and this documentation may
be invaluable in determining how reliable the work is as historic evidence. Audio and video interviews are additional source for this background information.

With the vast proliferation of fan magazines and general entertainment magazines in recent years there has been an exponential increase in the quantity of publicity and interview material available on
any major film release or popular television series, and it will have to
be assessed to determine whether it is actually worth the cost of filing,
housing, and servicing. The substantive value of this material appears
to decline in proportion to the volume available. The challenge to the
archivist is to ensure that related documentation on works that may not
have been popular successes but are nevertheless important cultural
contributions are not lost amid the outpouring on transient blockbust-
ers.

The archival value of scrapbooks of clippings is eminently debat-
able. A great deal will depend on the age of the clippings, their relevance to the moving images in the collection, and the relative rarity of
the material.

Audio and Video Interviews. In the past ten years there has been
a substantial increase in the use of audiovisual media to publicize film
and television productions. Radio and television interviews and background stories on moving image productions have become another vo-

luminous source for related documentation. They range from relatively valueless exchanges designed to showcase personality and the marketable aspects of the production to quite serious commentary on the work, the creative process, and the image-maker's intentions. Where they embody opinions and information that adds to the documentation on the work, they should be acquired. A more recent development is the interviews prepared for DVD re-releases of films. If the DVD is acquired, and it should be if it contains material not included in the original release version as acquired by the archives, then this ancillary documentation will automatically be acquired as well.

Additional Resources in DVD Releases. The *trailer* used to be the only production associated with the release of a motion picture that occasionally offered shots that were not in the film as released. It is now becoming common to find interviews, behind the camera production sequences, sequences that were edited out of the theatrical release version, and even alternative endings in the digital video version of the film. These are valuable resources for the study of the film, especially the extended release versions that are styled the *director's cut*, the version that was edited under the control of the director (or the producer if that is where creative control rested during production) before the work was tested with the public and altered, cut for length because it would be difficult to market, or otherwise re-edited to meet the perceived demands of the marketplace.

Digital Files and Related Software. The digital files associated with computer animation and special effects from major motion pictures are useless unless the software that enables them to be viewed is also acquired and preserved. In many cases the programming will have to be copied to some standard format adopted by the archives. Protocols for doing this are being formulated for electronic records of all types and moving image archivists should investigate the efforts to establish national and international standards before developing standalone systems.

Assessing the monetary value of related documentation is easier for stills, posters, and scripts because there is an established market for these through retail outlets specializing in film and television documentation, galleries (for posters), and through actual and virtual (Internet) auction sales. The usual factors of rarity and popular demand apply. Determining the value of printed material is more difficult. Again, age, subject, organization, and completeness are factors in assessing a collection. Individual items are even more difficult to assess. The value of

documentation on film or video is generally linked to issues of ownership and copyright, and there is unlikely to be any benchmarks in the
marketplace. Placing a value on material that was probably recorded off
air illegally is decidedly problematical!

In assessing all related documentation the general rule is that the
higher the value placed on the production, the higher the value placed
on the related documentation. This is not always the case, however.
The principle that old age must be respected holds for related documentation as well. Any material documenting the first twenty-five years of
cinema or the first ten years of television is likely to be of value. In
other cases the publicity campaign for an otherwise mediocre film may
be so innovative and effective that it merits retention. In still other
cases, the artists, photographers, or writers associated with the campaign may be significant enough in their own right to justify retaining
the documentation.

Chapter 6

Monetary Appraisal

Assessing the monetary value of moving image documents is an oner-
ous responsibility that has been thrust on archivists in recent years.
With acquisitions that can range from 70mm master elements for a $40
million dollar feature film production to an amateur cinematographer's
8mm *home movie* produced at a cost of $40, and everything in between,
placing a monetary value on such disparate materials is challenging.
The experience to date, primarily an attempt to set a price per foot of
film or per minute of videotape on broad categories of moving images,
has been generally unsatisfactory for both donors and archivists.

The stimulus has been the tax advantages that governments have introduced to promote the donation of works of art, heritage artifacts, and
documents of all kinds to designated institutions for the benefit of all
citizens. There is no question that such legislation has been tremendously successful as an incentive for donations. As Aaron Milrad observed: "Whether a donor's impetus is social standing or a genuine
desire to share the works with the designated institutions, its members,
and the general public for the greater good, any tax regime that does
not recognize the benefit to the community of such donations is short-
sighted and ultimately harmful to the nation it serves."[1] The social
benefit remains equally high if the donor's impetus is simply the tax
savings.

The irony inherent in the archivist's uneasiness in relation to monetary appraisal is that the taxation legislation in both the U.S. and Canada stresses that both the donor *and* the archivist should maintain an
arm's length relationship in the valuation of significant gifts of cultural
property. The role of the archivist was to negotiate a deed of gift (frequently to replace a deposit agreement, and in the process to resolve
any ownership issues), carry out an *archival* appraisal, describe the material if necessary, and prepare a statement on the cultural significance
of the donation as part of the application. Archivists, however, are also

expected to confirm the competency of the professional appraisers, to "protect the reputation of their institution" in the application for tax credits,"[2] and, in some jurisdictions, to actually carry out appraisals that fall below a given threshold in monetary value. From that perspective the arm's length is somewhat shorter.

The deed of gift (or whatever form the transfer of property takes) should be the starting point of every monetary appraisal. Does the donor own the work? Possession does not necessarily imply ownership, and as Milrad points out, "anyone who obtains objects or goods from a thief can have title and ownership to those objects and goods no greater than the title held by the thief."[3] This may appear to be glaringly obvious, but it is surprising how many institutions have neglected to learn the *provenance* of the works they acquired, or have even made an attempt to establish the history of the *title* to the works. The courts, apparently, take a dim view of *willful blindness*.

Because moving images are generally distributed through rental or leasing agreements rather than sold outright, and because of the copyright issues that restrict the uses to which the custodian of the physical property can legitimately put the documents, it has proved to be extremely difficult to establish *fair market value* under any broad definition of the term. In the absence of actual transactions at auction, for example, such monetary assessment can only be rough estimates based on the value placed on comparable documentation in other media.

There is a widely accepted definition of fair market value based on a number of legal rulings that was, perhaps, most clearly stated by Mr. Justice Cattanach in 1973:

> The statute does not define the expression "fair market value," but the expression has been defined in many different ways depending generally on the subject matter that the person seeking to define it had in mind. I do not think it necessary to attempt an exact definition of the expression as used in the statute other than to say that words must be construed in accordance with the common understanding of them. That common understanding I take to mean the *highest* price an asset might reasonably be expected to bring if sold by the owner in the normal method applicable to the asset in question in the ordinary course of business in a market not exposed to any undue stresses and composed of willing buyers and sellers dealing at arm's length and under no compulsion to buy or sell. I would add that the foregoing understanding as I have expressed it in a general way includes what I conceive to be the essential element; that is an open and unrestricted market in which the price is hammered out between willing and informed buyers and sellers

on the anvil of supply and demand. These definitions are equally appli-
cable to "fair market value" and "market value" as it is doubtful if the
word "fair" adds anything to the words "market value."[4]

Given the absence of *willing buyers and sellers*, appraisers of moving images have been forced to adopt other criteria such as *research
value*; the potential uses scholars will make of the material in years to
come, *historical value*, the role the material can play in helping write
the history of the family, community, or society that the material documents; and *cultural value*, a value that embodies all the others and
implies as well that every work reflects the civilization that produced it
and, in that way, has value.

These *values* are largely subjective, of course, and applying them
may result in wide variations in the valuations that result. This is not to
say that they are not valid approaches to valuation, but it should be
clear that a more objective approach would be easier to defend in a
court of law.

One more objective approach is *comparable market value*, an attempt to locate market prices for material that can be legitimately compared with the works being valued. This is easier when dealing with
individual works of art that are sold through dealers and at auction on a
regular basis. The work in hand may not have changed hands in such a
market, but similar works by the same artist, or by artists whose works
are generally ranked by experts as equivalent in quality or artistic importance, may have, and have thus established a "market value." Comparative market value is widely used in appraising *cel set-ups*, original
art work from animation films, as these are marketed and sold at auction around the world. Animation "art" along with posters is one aspect
of moving image production that was until recently routinely divorced
from the production files of the films and videos themselves and found
their way into the fine art market via dealers and auctions.

In an effort to arrive at a completely objective approach to the
valuation of film and video collections, appraisers have argued that the
minimum value of the collection should be the "replacement value."
This is not the same concept as that applied for insurance purposes,
which is a valuation based on the estimated cost of replacing the goods
lost with equivalent goods.

In dealing with film and video collections there can be no equivalent goods if the original *master* material (the original negative or other
primary source material) and the copies have been lost. One cannot re-
produce a motion picture even if cost was no object. As with any work

of art, the final result will be another work of art, no matter how faithful the creators tried to be to the original. In fact, the relationship between the actual cost of production for a professional film or video and the cost of the material that records that production is so tenuous that "cost of production," another approach to valuation, had never been applied to moving image collection.

With these collections replacement value is essentially the answer to the question: "What would the institution have had to pay in order to acquire a copy of the material deposited?" This is assumed to be the laboratory cost of "manufacturing" the copies from the surviving material at the time the collection was deposited.

The problem, and there are several problems associated with this approach, is to determine what technology should be employed to produce the copies, and what exactly, from the array of production materials that may be available, should the receiving institution have copied in order to protect the work(s) in the long term.

Determining what should be copied should be decided on the basis of the *archival* appraisal that should take place *before* the monetary appraisal. This assessment of *archival value* should result in a detailed inventory that specifies what material meets the collecting mandate and the selection criteria of the receiving institution. In many cases where the donor is the production organization, the collection will contain every image and piece of recorded sound that was assembled for the final editing of the work, and much of that may be superfluous to the requirements of the receiving institution. The premise should be to decide what is needed to protect and preserve the work and not to attempt to retain everything that might be needed to reconstruct the work, if that were possible.

There are those who will argue that every element used in the production of a significant work of art (film or video) should be retained, that the archivist should not presume to dictate what elements have value. These arguments have been discussed in chapter 1, and the conclusion is that if selection is necessary it should be carried out in as rational, as consistent, as objective, and as defensible manner as possible; that when operating with public funds (always limited) it is irresponsible to try to save every element associated with one film or video while hundreds more are not protected in any way.

Zapruder Film

As many of the issues surrounding the monetary appraisal of moving issues were highlighted in the legal dispute on the value of what is arguably the most famous piece of film in the world, it is worthwhile looking at the disposition of the Zapruder film in some detail.

On November 22, 1963, Abraham Zapruder, a Dallas businessman, went downtown to see the motorcade of President John F. Kennedy. He had his Bell & Howell 8mm camera with him and he captured the assassination of the President in 494 frames of Kodacolor II, a 6-foot length of film one-quarter of an inch wide, with a running time, when projected at the appropriate speed, of 26 seconds. Approximately 27 percent of the film shows police officers on motorcycles accompanying the motorcade, and approximately 73 percent contains images of the limousine in which the President was riding with clear images of the President at the time he was shot. Although the images on the film remain clear, the film has been broken in two places and spliced together, and one or two frames are missing from the camera original.[5]

The film was licensed by Mr. Zapruder to Time Inc. (publisher of *Time* and *Life* magazines) for $150,000, to be paid in installments of $25,000 each. The photos were sold to news magazines around the world by Time Inc., as well as appearing in *Time* and *Life*. After *Life* folded in 1972, the Zapruder family (Zapruder died in 1970) was allowed to buy back the original film *and the principal rights* for one dollar.

Shortly after the assassination and the murder of Lee Harvey Oswald by Jack Ruby on November 24, 1963, President Johnson appointed a commission headed by Chief Justice Earl Warren of the Supreme Court (President's Commission on the Assassination of President Kennedy, also known as the Warren Commission) to investigate the matter. The Zapruder film was a vital piece of the evidence that the Commission considered in reaching their conclusion that the assassination was the work of a lone gunman and that the gunman was Lee Harvey Oswald. This decision is still being challenged by historians, private investigators, and filmmakers (*JFK* [1991], directed by Oliver Stone) who maintain that there were two or more assassins, and that the assassination was the result of a conspiracy that has not yet been revealed. The Zapruder film is at once the most complete recording of President Kennedy's assassination and a challenging historic document that, over the past thirty-nine years, has been the focus of dozens of attempts to answer the various questions surrounding the death of the President.

After securing the copyright in the film Zapruder's family (wife Lillian, son Henry, and daughter Myrna) transferred ownership to LMH Company, a Texas general partnership. In 1978 the LMH Company deposited the film with the National Archives and Records Administration for storage and safekeeping. The Zapruders continued to exercise their copyright rights, however, and between 1976 and 1997 the film earned $878,997 in reproduction rights for the Zapruder family. When Lillian Zapruder Grossman died in 1994, her estate reported to the Internal Revenue Service that the film "has an appraised copyright and licensing value of $512,000 based on the income generated from licensing activities."[6]

On August 1, 1988, the Assassination Research Board directed that the Zapruder film be transferred to the Records Collection within the National Archives and Records Administration. That same day the government seized the film itself, *but not the copyright for the film.* The seizure was pursuant to special legislation enacted by the U.S. Congress, and under the Fifth Amendment to the U.S. Constitution the owners of the film, LMH Company, were entitled to just compensation. To determine the just compensation, the United States and LMH entered into an arbitration agreement, dated October 15, 1998, under which three arbitrators were selected to determine the amount the government must pay as *just compensation* for its seizure of the film in the public interest.

The arbitration agreement actually stipulated that the amount determined by the arbitrators could not be more than $30 million, a sum which the arbitrators described as "apparently a reflection of the fact that there is no readily apparent precedent to govern the determination of value in a situation such as this."

In attempting to establish a value for the film, the arbitrators received and reviewed prehearing briefs, examined numerous affidavits from appraisers and art auctioneers, and conducted two full days of hearings in Washington, D.C., at which appraisers and auctioneers for both sides testified.

The first point clarified in the decision was that the appraised value of the film as reported to the Internal Revenue Service in 1994 was a reflection of the value of the film *for purposes of licensing activities* and not a determination of value for the film *as an historic object.*

The second point was that because LMH Company retained control of the copyright the arbitrators determined that the government should only pay for the physical property and not for any collateral interests. The government did not dispute that the camera original of the Zapruder film has value as a collectible property, and its experts variously attributed values of $748,000 and $1,000,000 to the film.[7]

The LMH appraisers described the film as an *icon* and attributed values ranging from $25,000,000 to no less than $40,000,000.[8] Their rationale centered on the fact that the film was unique, that it was known around the world as *the Zapruder film*, and that it had extraordinary value in the open market because of its relationship to the late President and to an historic event that is generally regarded as one of the most important events in twentieth century American history.

LMH had also claimed that the seizure of the film had resulted in a loss of income of at least $10,000,000. The arbitrators rejected that claim on the grounds that lost profits from business opportunities foreclosed by government seizures of this type are not subject to compensation (*United States v. General Motors Corp., 323 U.S. 373, 379, [1945]*), nor are any business opportunities that would have resulted from collateral interests such as licensing, which LMH could still exercise as they controlled the copyright in the film.

The arbitrators focused exclusively on the *fair market value* of the physical property, the 6 feet of camera original that Abraham Zapruder exposed on that fateful day, the price that a willing seller and a willing buyer would hammer out in an unrestricted market. Appraisers for the government argued that there was no proved marketplace for the sale of camera original film. Appraisers for LMH argued that in the absence of such a market the arbitrators should judge the value of the film *as comparable to* the value of a number of well-known items of personal property sold in the past.

The problem with comparisons, argued the arbitrators, was that you cannot *predict with assurance* that the prices paid in the past for arguably similar items of personal property would be obtained today. The lack of an established market prompted the arbitrators to reject consideration of particular sales alleged to be comparable "if those sales appear questionable in light of the market as a whole." That view, the appropriateness of applying a single auction sale price as a general indicator of comparable values has been noted by several commentators on monetary appraisals. Any one price may have resulted from a set of conditions (rival collectors who are so competitive that the bidding is no longer rational) that probably will never be repeated and does not reflect the *market value* for comparable works. Aaron Milrad argues that auction results are "no more that one indicator of a price achieved at a particular time and place of a particular object of personal property."[9]

Witnesses for both parties recognized that although many historic films exist, there is little market history documenting the sale of camera original film. In fact no examples were presented in evidence. Films of the 1934 assassination of King Alexander of Yugoslavia, and films of the murder of national leaders such as Anwar Sadat, Rajiv Gandhi, Yitzhak Rabin, Benigno Aquino, and Robert Kennedy exist, but the camera originals have not been offered for sale. Films of famous events were also considered—the bombing of Pearl Harbor, the Wright Brothers' flight at Kitty Hawk, and the explosion of the dirigible *Hindenberg*—and judged irrelevant as well, as there were no recorded sales of camera originals.

It is difficult to understand why the arbitrators bothered to review somewhat contemporaneous *historic* film from the sixties—monks immolating themselves in Vietnam, the summary street execution of a prisoner by a South Vietnamese officer, the image of a Vietnamese child running naked to escape the effects of napalm being dropped on her village, the crowds at Woodstock, a student kneeling beside the body of another student at Kent State University, the scene on the balcony after the assassination of Martin Luther King—when none of the appraisers documented a sale of a camera original for any of these iconic images. The government witnesses maintained that the reason there are no sales recorded for these and other referential images is that they are valued for their content, not as *relics or icons*, and that the desire for film content has been satisfied by access through archives and stock footage libraries.

Despite those reservations the arbitrators proceeded to consider auction sales results for works whose associations and considerable historic and cultural significance had assigned to them extraordinary value—President Eisenhower's D-Day Order ($200,000), President Lincoln's "House Divided" speech ($1.5 million), a broadsheet of the Declaration of Independence ($2.4 million). Both sides agreed that a substantial valuation was warranted in this case of the Zapruder film, but one issue remained: how much?

Although both the government and LMH Company relied on qualified appraisers of historic documents and artifacts, the arbitrators concluded that the opinions of LMH's qualified appraisers *and* "undisputed world-class experts when it came to the role of auction houses and the process of auctioning to the public famous historical items" should prevail.[10] Their experience with Sotheby's and Christy's appeared to carry weight with the arbitrators in the absence of testimony by the government's appraisers to counter their predictions on what the Zapruder film would bring in an open auction.

The LMH appraisers started high, with one concluding that the film was worth at least $25 million, and speculating that it could go for double or even triple that amount. The comparables here were works of art by Van Gogh, Monet, and Picasso. Another selected the *Codex Leicester* of Leonardo da Vinci as a benchmark and argued that if Bill Gates could be induced to bid $30 million for the *Codex* than the Zapruder film would probably sell for $25 million.

The government appraisers did not contradict this testimony, which after all was only speculation, and offered instead an argument based on the fact that the film changed hands in 1963 for $150,000, which computed to $780,000 in 1999 dollars. Their view, summed up in a minority report (the panel of three split two to one), was that the value of the film lay in the images, not in the 6-foot strip of celluloid that the government seized in 1992. The minority report conceded that the value of the film would be greatly enhanced through association with President Kennedy, but it pointed out that in a recent sale of Kennedy memorabilia the highest price paid was $1.4 million for the 1776 desk upon which President Kennedy had signed the Nuclear Test Ban Treaty. Even allowing a fourfold increase in the value the film established at the only time it changed hands in the marketplace—the $780,000 in 1999 dollars that *Time Inc.* paid in 1963—the value of the film, they argued, was closer to $3.5 million than the $25 million proposed by the LMH appraisers.

The minority report also took exception to the use of great works of art as comparables since the attributes of these works—the status of the artist, their aesthetic appeal, their sales and ownership history, and the undeniable fact that there can be no real comparison between the original and a copy in terms of responding to the image—have little bearing on the value of the camera original of the Zapruder film as a historic artifact.

The arbitrators awarded LMH Company $16 million, a sum that appears to be close to the mid-point between the government's estimate of $1 million and the maximum of $30 million set when the arbitration panel was established. The reaction to the award was somewhat hostile, with many commentators arguing that the film should simply have been confiscated by the government as an invaluable historic document and as a crucial piece of evidence in the ongoing controversy surrounding the assassination. Even those conceding that the government had no right to seize the film without adequate compensation argued that $16 million was too high an award. The issue that troubled most archivists and curators is that the government did not gain control of the copyright as a result of the award. Under the terms of the settlement all use of the images, aside from research on the premises of the National Archives, had to be approved by LMH Company.

In January 2000, the Zapruder family donated a first-generation copy of the film *and the copyright* to the Sixth Floor Museum at Dealey Plaza in Dallas, which is located in the Texas School Book Depository building from which, as the Warren Commission concluded, the fatal shots were fired. Assuming that the film is treated as an unpublished work under the Berne Convention and the copyright is protected for seventy years following the death of the creator, because Abraham Zapruder died in 1970, the film will not be in the public domain until 2040.

Appraisal Methodology

The Zapruder film arbitration hearings illustrate the key role played by appraisers in assessing monetary value. One can argue that the Zapruder family was awarded at least $10 million more than they would have been if not for the testimony *and status* of their appraisers. The testimony highlights the importance of qualified appraisers in assessing value, and in particular when monetary value has to be assessed in dealing with government agencies on tax credits for gifts to institutions designated as qualified recipients under the taxation legislation of the jurisdictions in which they operate.

The first principle to be observed is that the appraisal should always be conducted at arm's length. Neither the donor nor the recipient institution should participate in carrying out the appraisal. This is essential if there are legal issues such as insurance policies or tax benefits involved. In Canada, for example, the Canadian Cultural Property Export Review Board (CCPERB) requires two *independent* appraisals for property whose estimated fair market value is more than $10,000 CAN. Below that sum one appraiser will do. The Board also accepts estimates of fair market value from committees of at least three appraisers for property of any value. The National Archival Appraisal Board (NAAB), established by the archival community in consultation with Revenue Canada, provides that service. The committees should consist of a dealer, an archivist/historian, and someone with any other expertise that may be appropriate. In dealing with audiovisual collections, the CCPERB suggests a committee comprising a professional appraiser with significant market experience, a producer or dealer, and a moving image archivist or historian.

The U.S. Internal Revenue Service (IRS) requires at least one estimate "from a qualified and reputable source" for any gift valued at more than $5,000, and a complete signed appraisal for any gift valued at more than $20,000. If the estimate is more than $50,000, the IRS must issue a *Statement of Value* before the claim is filed, which is based on the appraisals provided by the claimant and requires the payment of a $2,500 fee.

In the Canadian context there is a distinction made between gifts to charitable or designated nonprofit institutions, which do not have to meet certain criteria relating to "outstanding significance and national importance" and which offer slightly lesser tax advantages than those that do meet those criteria and are certified by the Canadian Cultural Property Export Review Board.

CCPERB insists that a thorough *archival* appraisal be carried out *before* a monetary appraisal is commissioned. This would appear to be an obvious first step for a recipient institution to take before agreeing to accept any donation. The archival appraisal should affirm that the work or works to be acquired meet the collecting mandate and the selection criteria of the institution and that a detailed inventory of the material to be accessioned has been compiled to facilitate the work of the appraiser.

It is important to note that a collection, or the production files of an image-maker, may contain material that has *archival* value as an integral element in a collection or *fonds* (loosely defined as the records of an administrative unit of government, a corporation, a family, or an individual, produced or received in carrying out their activities) and have little or no *monetary* value. The obvious point is that if the work, or an element that was used to produce the final work, has no *archival* value it should not be accessioned and therefore should not be included in the material to be appraised.

A checklist for an institution carrying out an *archival* appraisal prior to submitting a *monetary* appraisal of a moving image collection, as outlined by CCPERB[11], contains the following items. My comments are in brackets:

- ❑ degree to which a full physical inspection of the property has taken place [this implies an item-by-item description with physical assessments of each reel];
- ❑ scope and content of the property being accessioned [and whose fair market value is to be assessed];
- ❑ physical condition of the property and any urgent conservation measures that are required [factors which would affect the value of the gift];
- ❑ level of staff expertise available at the institution to process the material;
- ❑ ability of the institution to preserve the material in terms of adequate storage facilities, and appropriate temperature and humidity controls for film and videotape [combined with staff expertise above, and surveillance mechanisms and migration strategies below, the issue here is the institution's ability to protect the gift and to provide public access in the long term];
- ❑ surveillance mechanisms in place to monitor the material, including preventive and treatment strategies;
- ❑ migration strategy in place to cope with deteriorating and/or obsolescent recording formats;
- ❑ long-term preservation costs of the material, including migration to other formats, and whether it is able to absorb those costs;
- ❑ description of the cultural property in terms of title, provenance, years the property spans, whether the property is complete or constitutes an accrual, and the extent of the material;
- ❑ provide a copy of the donation agreement, or deed of gift, that fully describes the property to be donated in terms of what the recipient institution is retaining that establishes:
  - ❑ legal ownership of the property in question;
  - ❑ that an irrevocable gift is being made, without any conditions attached;

- ❏ the rights to be retained by the donor and the rights that are being transferred to the institution;
- ❏ provide a detailed finding aid which clearly describes the donation, and if this has been provided by the donor or a third party, whether it has been verified for accuracy;
- ❏ provide an explanation of the "outstanding significance and national importance" of the donation that addresses;
  - ❏ research value;
  - ❏ pertinence to the collecting mandate and collections already held by the recipient institution;
  - ❏ public access;
  - ❏ uniqueness.

Selecting an Appraiser

Finding a qualified appraiser of an audiovisual collection requires careful consideration. The guidelines that follow have been abstracted from *Appraising Audiovisual Media* by Steve Johnson, a publication of the Association for Educational Communications and Technology.[12] The U.S. Internal Revenue Service (IRS) defines both *qualified appraiser* and *qualified appraisals*. What the IRS expects is that the media appraiser should hold himself or herself out to the public as an appraiser of audiovisual media, and possess qualifications to appraise in his or her fields of audiovisual media.

The key point is that appraisers are independent professionals who have no personal interest in the object or collection of objects under evaluation. If they have had previous dealings with the donor or the custodial institution they should state so in their appraisal.

Some appraisers make a distinction between *valuation* and *appraisal*, reserving valuation for an overall assessment of cultural value and then using appraisal for a more technical assessment of the fair market value based on comparable values in the marketplace. As the assessment of fair market value should always embody cultural value, whether derived from a narrow historic research perspective, or from a broader cultural perspective, there is little purpose in maintaining a distinction and the two terms are used here interchangeably.

Appraisers should bring knowledge, experience, and integrity to the assignment. In North America they are often members of the American Society of Appraisers, the Appraisers Association of America, or the

International Society of Appraisers. These associations maintain rosters of members and can identify appraisers with the expertise required. It should be noted that even the largest of the societies may not be willing or able to test and certify their members. Certification for appraisers is a relatively new development and many appraisers have been *grand-fathered* as members without testing. A select group of appraisers specializing in media—film, video, sound recordings, and photography—have established the Media Appraisal Consultants network. Membership is based on peer recognition of their professional qualifications.

Many expert appraisers of audiovisual materials are not, however, professional appraisers. They have derived their knowledge of the content from years of study or teaching, or as custodians or image-makers. As long as they approach the task free of bias or prejudice, and free of any direct association with either the donor or the recipient institution, and they have an understanding of how the market for cultural property operates, they should be able to provide a valid and defensible evaluation of the donation.

All appraisers should appraise all items objectively, consistently, accurately, and clearly, holding all appraisals confidential. In 1987 various U.S. and Canadian professional associations created The Appraisal Foundation "to foster professionalism in appraising through the promotion of appraisal standards and the assessing of valuer qualifications."[13] The result was the development of the Uniform Standard of Professional Appraisal Practice (USPAP). The Foundation established the Appraiser Qualifications Board and the Appraisal Standards Board to implement standards for qualifications and for conduct, but these remain voluntary.

The ethics promulgated by USPAP are similar to those adopted by the Appraiser's Association of America. Members agree to abide by the Association's Code of Ethics that stresses the following:

❏ Every appraiser must sign and certify his or her appraisal.
❏ Every appraiser has the responsibility to contract for appraisal work only within his or her professional competence, and to call upon a qualified appraiser for that portion of the appraisal outside his or her expertise.
❏ All items of property within an appraisal must be appraised objectively, independent of outside influence,

and without any other motive or purpose other than stated in the appraisal.

❑ The appraiser must examine personally all items for appraisal [if at all possible], and must note items not personally examined.

❑ It is the appraiser's responsibility to keep all appraisals confidential, unless required by the owner, or by due process of law, to release such appraisal.

❑ Appraisers prepare appraisals under varying circumstances that can influence the valuation of the property. It is necessary to determine the nature and purpose of each appraisal in advance and to note its purpose.

Contents of the Appraisal

The purpose of the appraisal and the conditions under which it will be conducted, including the time frame, should all be clearly stated in the letter of engagement between the client (the donor or the institution) and the appraiser. Stating the purpose—valuation for taxation benefits associated with a gift to a charitable or nonprofit institution, valuation for insurance coverage, valuation before placing the work or works up for auction, etc.—is essential, and the appraiser will probably stipulate that the appraisal can only be used for that purpose. This is not to suggest that the valuation will change dramatically with a change in purpose, but the appraiser will draft the final report differently to meet the requirements of the agency or organization involved.

The letter of engagement will also, of course, state the fee for the appraisal, and whether it is an hourly or daily rate, or a flat fee, it should *never be contingent on the amount of the appraisal*. In fact, taxation authorities will insist on a statement signed by the appraiser to the effect: I have no present or future undisclosed financial interest in the appraised audiovisual media, and my fee for this appraisal is not contingent upon my evaluation in the appraisal.

The U.S. Internal Revenue Service checklist for a qualified appraisal is as follows:

❑ description of the audiovisual media that allows someone unfamiliar with it to recognize it as the property that has been donated;

❑   description of the physical condition of the media;

❑   donation date of the media, which is not necessarily the same as the date of either the appraisal report document or of the evaluation itself;

❑   terms of any agreement or understanding involving the donor concerning the use, sale, or disposition of the media contributed;

❑   name, address, and taxpayer identification of the qualified appraiser;

❑   qualifications of the appraiser, including background, experience, education, and membership in professional associations;

❑   purpose of the appraisal;

❑   date of the valuation of the media assets, not necessarily the same as the date of the report or of the donation;

❑   appraised fair market value of the audiovisual assets on the date of contribution;

❑   method of valuation used to determine the fair market value;

❑   specific basis for the valuation, if any, such as any specific comparable sales; and

❑   description of the fee arrangement between the donor and the appraiser.

It should be clear that it is the responsibility of the archives or custodial institution to either prepare or validate the inventory of collection. If the collection includes a complete descriptive inventory, whether or not it is machine readable, which would allow immediate access to the collection and thus save the recipient institution a great deal of time and money in processing the collection, this should add to its value. The Canadian Cultural Property Export Review Board does not allow the value of finding aids to be added to the value of property submitted for tax certification, but recognizes that such documentation has value and suggests that it be treated as a charitable gift.

There is a very wide range of film and video that is now being judged *archival* and valued accordingly. Even a partial list would include amateur films, usually on small gauge stock such as 8mm and Super 8mm, 16mm, or on consumer versions of videotape such as VHS or Beta ½ -inch videocassettes, and whose content can range from ordinary family life to the great events of our time; sponsored films or *in-*

dustrials, which were made to promote a product or persuade the public to support or oppose some legal, economic, or social issue; film and television commercials designed to sell products, services, or politicians; film or videotape recordings of debates, seminars, lectures, or interviews; test film from scientific experiments; footage documenting geographic, anthropologic and ethnographic expeditions; film and video produced as part of multimedia art or installations; independent/experimental image-makers who use *found footage* and/or distort images in the laboratory or by drawing/scratching directly on to the surface of the film; all the output from the film and television industries, *product* as diverse as news film, with and without commentary; news and current events commentary shows; documentaries; serial television; talk shows; sporting events; and short and feature-length fiction films.

All of these have value—a case can be made that every foot of film and every minute of video has some h*eritage value*—but the challenge is to determine *fair market value.* This would be inestimably easier if film and videotape productions, amateur or professional, were sold on the open market all the time. Unfortunately this is not the case, with very rare exceptions, and distribution in the commercial industry is through licensing agreements. As we have seen in the Zapruder case, when appraisers have to search for comparable values in the marketplace they have to reach for comparisons with other art objects, and very, very few moving images will stand up to that test.

Appraisal Process

There are only three basic approaches to the valuation of audiovisual media:

The Cost Approach

The *cost of production* has never proved to be a useful approach to the appraisal of audiovisual collections. The prime obstacle has been the vast disparity between the cost of production and the assessed value of the material when divorced from the potential revenue it can generate when first commercially broadcast or distributed theatrically. Production cost has no relation to *heritage value* as well. Because a feature film cost $60 million to produce, and perhaps another $15 million to advertise and distribute, has very little impact on the *archival* advertise and distribute, has very little impact on the *archival value* when compared, for example, with a documentary on the civil rights movement in the sixties that contains unique footage. Even in the rare case when prints of feature films (usually films that are already in the public domain in the U.S.) are offered for sale, the price set is based on the condition of the print, rarity, and established demand for the work of the director or the leading players, and bears no relation to production costs.

Revenue Generation

Revenue generation comes into play when the audiovisual donation includes the transfer of copyright and ownership rights that will allow the recipient institution to *market* the material through direct sales of stock footage or through the licensing of broadcasts or theatrical exhibition. It also comes into play, of course, if the material donated is out of copyright and still marketable. The problem with this approach is the determination of what these rights are worth. Unlike the case of the inventory of a shop or a manufacturer, where the value of the goods can be determined by the either the price paid for them, or by established market prices, and the goods can only be sold once, film and video can be licensed repeatedly and copies of stock footage can be sold indefinitely.

There does not appear to be an acceptable formula for predicting revenue that will be generated by exercising the rights being acquired. If the organization that is making the donation has been in the business of selling stock footage, the tax authorities would probably accept the average of the past three years of sales as an appropriate valuation. The question is whether the valuation should embrace the revenue to be generated for only one year or should that be extended out for three years, five years, ten years, or more?

Where the donor has not sold or licensed the material before, predicting revenue is even more problematical. Comparisons can be made with similar footage offered for sale elsewhere, but deriving an average cost per minute (stock shots are usually priced per minute of screen time) can be difficult. The price will vary with the purpose for which the footage is being sold: the price for educational use, for example, will be substantially less than that for unlimited worldwide commercial television use. Prices also vary with the quantity of footage being sold, and in the final analysis all prices for any significant quantity of material are negotiable.

Replacement Cost

The most objective method to determine *fair market value* for moving image donations is based on the answer to one question: what would the heritage institution have been willing to pay for the collection if it had not been donated? The question assumes that the collection falls within the collecting mandate of the institution and that its *archival* value, as opposed to its *monetary* value, has been thoroughly assessed.

In the mid-seventies, when the National Archives of Canada's moving image acquisition program was still being developed, the archivists proposed that the absolute minimum valuation that should be placed on a donation of 35mm motion picture film should be $1.00 per foot. This was somewhat arbitrary but was, in fact, not too far off what it would have cost on average, at that time, to acquire a 35mm negative, a 35mm interpositive, and a 35mm print from a laboratory. If the original source were a 35mm print, the intermediate, of course, would be a duplicate negative. This *replacement cost* was construed as the *fair market value* of the donation.

The difference between *purchase* and *replacement* should be clear. *Purchase* implies that there is a negative in a laboratory from which a print can be struck for institutional use. *Replacement* implies that the institution will have to pay for an intermediate before the print can be manufactured.

Based on that premise, one that Revenue Canada and the IRS have accepted as a reasonable approach to valuation, a *cost replacement* methodology has been developed that is used to assess the value of the *physical property* in an audiovisual collection donated to a heritage institution. The costs are now the actual costs that laboratories charge for the manufacture or transfer of various types of moving images, whether film or videotape, analog or digital.

One of the concerns with this method is the necessity to conduct a rigorous *archival* appraisal of the collection *before* carrying out the *monetary* appraisal. The *archival* appraisal should first determine what the institution would normally have acquired in order to protect each production in the long term and to provide public access, and the *monetary* appraisal should apply *only* to those elements of the donation.

To illustrate the distinction, take the case of a university in Canada that recently accepted the donation of a 1-hour television show, an adaptation of a literary classic. The elements included three 1-inch videotape recordings of the entire broadcast, four copies of 16mm duplicate negative picture, five copies of 16mm magnetic sound track, six copies of 16mm negative picture, two copies of 16mm print, six copies of 35mm magnetic track, three copies of 35mm negative, and one copy of a VSH ½ -inch cassette. Two appraisers valued the replacement cost of this material at $15,000, but it is highly unlikely that any heritage institution in this country would purchase that many elements in order to protect the title and to provide public access.

It may be that the recipient institution in the case above had assigned *archival* value to some of these elements (and heritage institutions often accept material because the donor insists that the entire collection be kept intact), but if the elements are redundant they do not have *monetary* value when applying the *cost replacement* method.

The problem is compounded when the appraiser *enhances* the valuation of a collection on the grounds that it is of particular cultural or historical significance. If the *base* for this enhancement is the value placed on *all* the *physical* property—the cultural factor can be as high as 100 percent, a doubling of the estimate—the result is an estimate that is significantly inflated. One factor to consider is that the valuation for cultural value should really take place independently and should not be calculated as a percentage of the replacement cost. That it frequently is so calculated is a matter of convenience rather than sound appraisal methodology.

Assessing historic or cultural value on the basis of the *cost replacement* estimate introduces a highly subjective factor into what should be a relatively objective methodology. One appraiser uses "subjective additions or subtractions according to the success of the production, the cast and crew involved, national and international exposure, awards earned, the presence of a *master* copy, and completeness (or incompleteness) of the element package."

There is another aspect of the *cost replacement* method that should be considered. If the institution accepting the gift will be required to invest a substantial amount of money in order to preserve the material being donated, should this have a negative impact on the valuation? In 1969 the United States Court of Appeal, Federal Circuit, disallowed a contribution of $8,394,000 claimed by Transamerica Corporation as a result of the donation to the Library of Congress of 1,000 feature films and 2,000 short films produced by Warner Bros. and Monogram Pictures before 1950. The films were are all on nitrate stock and the gift was restricted to the physical property. The Court noted that while the Library spent more than $1 million to convert the films to safety stock, Transamerica "received the right, to the exclusion of other members of the public, to obtain access to the Library's safety film for commercial purposes in perpetuity." The Court concluded that the value of Transamerica's gift should be reduced by at least the amount the Library had spent in preserving the gift.

While this issue has surfaced in other cases of moving image donations, and in donations of fine art where the recipient institution has had to spend considerable sums to stabilize a work that was deteriorating, it is often ignored in moving image donations. Part of the problem is that the institution will probably have to physically treat the material in order to manufacture a reference copy for public access, and the line between preservation transfers and public service processing is rather thin.

Despite problems in applying the methodology consistently, the *cost replacement* method remains the most objective approach to the *monetary* appraisal of audiovisual collections. The method should only be applied, however, after a thorough *archival* appraisal has been carried out and a very precise and detailed inventory of the collection has been prepared. The inventory should allow the institution to determine exactly what material it requires in order to ensure the long-term preservation of the acquisitions and to provide public access.

Appraisers should keep in mind that *cost replacement* is a method of calculating the *monetary* value of a collection that has been designated as having *archival* value, and that not everything in the collection necessarily has *monetary* value. The donor and the institution may have good reasons for wanting to keep the collection intact and complete, but the appraiser should only assign value to those elements the institution would have acquired, in the absence of a donation, in order to preserve and protect the production and to provide public access.

Fundamental Archival Rights

While they are seldom evaluated, there are certain other rights that should be transferred to the archives by deed of gift or deposit agreement. The first, and most fundamental, is the right to have custody of the *physical* property. This can be either a deposit (long-term loan) or an outright gift. It is in the effort to change *deposits* into *gifts*—the depositor usually reserves the right to withdraw the material with or without some compensation to the archives—that the tax deduction incentive is promoted. Donors have to understand that *ownership of the physical property must be transferred* before the material can be appraised for this purpose

The second right, and one that many heritage institutions insist on before they will accept custody, is the right to make the material accessible on the premises of the institution for research purpose. Recent changes to the Copyright Act in both the U.S. and Canada gave designated institutions the right to make copies in order to protect the work *and* to make it accessible. The right to provide access is frequently extended to include not-for-profit exhibition of the material on the premises of or under the auspices of the custodial institution, although this is still contested in many jurisdictions and in many cases must be approved under separate agreements with the donors and the copyright owners.

The right to provide access and the right to copy the material is, in effect, a limited transfer of *intellectual* property with great *archival* value but no *monetary* value. The custodial institution may charge a fee for access, but that is always construed as a means of recovering either the administrative costs in providing the service or the laboratory costs in making reference copies, or both.

The third right is a more substantial transfer of *intellectual* property. This normally involves the right of the institution to make copies of the material available to third parties for use off the premises of the institution, for either nonprofit or commercial purposes. The institution may add any or all of three charges that will generate revenue to sustain the activities of the institution: the first is the cost of making the copies; the second is the cost of administering the service, which may incorporate costs associated with marketing the service; and the third is a royalty fee that will vary with the use to which the third party, the client, intends to put the material supplied. This can range from modest royalty fees for educational use in nonprofit educational institutions to quite substantial fees ($5,000/minute is not uncommon) for commercial use involving worldwide television sales. In almost all cases this right is limited to the sale of *stock shots*—shots or sequences taken from the edited film or from unedited material. The commercial exploitation of the entire work is almost always retained by the donor or is held by a third party for broadcast, video rental and sales, or theatrical exhibition.

Calculating the value of this third type of transfer is difficult because it always relies on a projection of *potential* revenue. The *assumption* is that the donor would have realized this return if the *physical* and *intellectual* property had not been donated.

There are, as we have seen, three problems in calculating revenue generation method: 1) what is the average price at which the *units* will be sold?; 2) what is the projected annual volume of sales?; and 3) for how many years should that projection be calculated in order to arrive at an approximate value for the donation? If the donor can provide evidence of the volume of sales and/or the dollars earned in the past three years, this task is simplified. In many cases, however, the donor has not been engaged in stock shot sales. There is no solid evidence on which potential revenue generation can be based. Information on revenue generated from sale of comparable material must be used, and these comparisons are never very precise. The old maxim in Hollywood used to be that "a tree was a tree," and therefore any tree would do. It is doubtful whether basing an evaluation on the premise that a shot is a shot, and all are equal in value, will carry you very far in a court of law.

Even where there is hard evidence of revenue potential (generally speaking for a minimum of three years prior to the donation) it is problematic whether those revenue levels will be sustained in the next three years. The stock shot market has become very competitive internationally in recent years with online access becoming the norm. Recent mergers have resulted in a few, very large *commercial libraries* dominating the field. Predicting demand in the immediate future, even three to five years, is, therefore, highly speculative. And what constitutes a *fair* number of years in projecting potential revenue? Some appraisers argue three years, others seven, and in rare cases twenty-five years has been proposed. The determination of this vital factor will obviously have a drastic effect on the total valuation if this approach is adopted.

One last factor that must be kept in mind in estimating the value of transfers of intellectual property rights is determining exactly what rights the custodial institution actually acquired. The deed of gift should clearly state what these rights are, whether they are exclusive or nonexclusive—if the donor, or a third party, will also sell stock shots from the same material, for example, this will sharply reduce the value of that right—and, most important, that the donor actually held the rights (unencumbered by other contractual obligations) that are being transferred. This may require legal interpretation where collections have changed hands two or three times before finally being donated.

The *provenance* of the collection, or of individual works in the collection—the history of the works since they were created—becomes an important factor.

The custodial institution has a major responsibility in assembling the available documentation that describes the collection in terms of physical property, the content, the context in which it was produced, and its custodial history from the time it was created. This will help the appraiser in assessing the monetary value, particularly in attempting to assess the research, historic, and cultural value of the collection.

Animation

Animation collections represent a new set of challenges to the appraiser. The edited film or video is seldom a special problem as the same methodology as that applied to other types of film or video will serve. The real challenge lies in the artwork created for animation, the 1,200 to 1,500 hundred drawings, cels, and backgrounds, which are required for a half-hour of animation.

There is general consensus that there is now an established market for animation art, and one that is growing rapidly as more and more producers of animation enter the market and begin designing *product* to meet the demands of the marketplace. The works of art that are the product for this market are cel set-ups—painted acetate transparencies mounted and framed with the appropriate background art—that are *animated* to tell the story. Until fairly recently the artwork for the transparencies and the backgrounds were all hand-painted. This technique is being rapidly replaced by computer animation that is not only less expensive but allows manipulations of the images that are difficult if not impossible with the older technique. This will inevitably raise the value of hand-painted cels, but it is still unclear from the marketplace what impact this will have on the price of cels, as there is such a vast quantity of hand-drawn cels available.

The market now accepts both hand-drawn and computer generated images, but generally values the hand-drawn cel set-ups much higher and assigns the highest values to hand-drawn cel set-ups from "classic" or vintage animated films—cel set-ups with original backgrounds from Disney's *Snow White* (1937) are probably the most expensive in the marketplace, with one selling at auction a few years ago for $40,000. Producers now also issue *limited editions* of cel set-ups, hand painted or very high-quality copies, usually signed by the animator, to satisfy the market.

The animation market is well established, but still very much in transition and operating at various levels from entertainment media stores (Disney, Warner Bros., MGM) in malls, dealing primarily in reproductions of classic cartoon personalities (Bugs Bunny, Mickey Mouse, etc.) to specialized collector dealers. There are a number of animation galleries around the world that specialize in animation art and many more galleries that carry animation art along with other forms of art.

The advent of Internet marketing has both expanded and destabilized the market with hundreds of sites such as e-Bay and Yahoo! offering animation at prices that can vary from $10 to $10,000! As in the larger market for fine art, the market responds to economic conditions and prices can drop as well as rise. Some of the largest auction houses (Christie's, Sotheby's) that were heavily involved with animation art in the nineties have now reduced their involvement or are restricting their involvement to very special sales. The market appears to be in a constant state of flux.

Setting the price for cel set-ups is relatively straightforward if there have been sales of works from the same series featuring the same characters. Prices do fluctuate—it is unlikely that cel set-ups from *The Simpsons* will reach the same level as when the series first became highly popular and achieved cult status with thousands of fans—but it should be possible to derive *average* prices in the *current* marketplace that can be used to value the collection.

It becomes more problematic when there are no sales, or insufficient sales to establish an average price, and prices for *comparable* animation art must be used. Comparative pricing is always speculative unless one argues that all animation art is equal, on the face of it an absurd proposition and one that is disproved by the wide range of prices at which animation art is offered in the current marketplace. In fact, there are wide variations in the pricing determined by appraisers presumably working from the same dealer catalogs and auction records.

There are also significant differences among appraisers on the volume of artwork from a given production that is *marketable*. Some appraisers hold, as do most reputable dealers, that only *original* hand-drawn cels combined with *original* backgrounds are marketable at premium prices, the top of the market. All other cel set-ups are discounted by 30 to 50 percent Other appraisers contend that cel set-ups with *cop-*

ied backgrounds can be marketed at the same price. As the number of *original* backgrounds is very small in relation to the number of cels, this difference of opinion in *reading* the market can lead to substantial differences in appraised values.

There are also marked differences in the values assigned to the drawings that are the basis of the cel artwork. Some appraisers contend that all the drawings are marketable in a range of prices. Others maintain that only a very limited quantity of key drawings are marketable.

Pricing is a critical factor in applying the *market data comparison* method because of the vast number of artworks associated with each production. There are between twelve and fifteen thousand cels created for each half-hour of animation, and some of the collections from animation studios donated to custodial institutions in recent years have contained more than 250,000 items. Even slight shifts in the estimate of average price per unit, and in the number of marketable units, will have a very marked impact on the total valuation.

This impact, which has been called *the power of the multiplier,* can lead to severe distortions in the appraisal. One item overpriced by $50.00 may be tolerable, twenty thousand items overpriced by the same amount is not! In one case re-assessed by the Canadian Cultural Property Export Review Board the three appraisers not only disagreed on the average price, but on the quantity of cel set-ups that could be derived from the production files. One appraiser determined, by sampling the collection, that only 10 percent of the cels were marketable, and found that there were twenty thousand potential cel set-ups in the production files for a single series of animated films made for children's television. Setting the average fair market price at $250 per cel set-up, the appraiser estimated the value of the collection at five million dollars. A second appraiser, adopting a more conservative approach, but also based on sampling the collection, determined that only 6 percent of the cels were marketable and set the average fair market price at $200. His estimation of the value of the collection was $2.4 million. Such is the power of the multiplier!

There is a tendency to assume that if there is a market for one cel set-up from a production there will be a market for any number of cel set-ups. This ignores the diminishing returns to be experienced in a saturated market. In fact, the issue of *block discount* has surfaced in court cases involving investors acquiring significant numbers of works from one artist at bargain prices and then having them appraised at much higher values as gifts to custodial institutions.[14] The argument by the taxation authorities has been that if the works had been placed on the market all at one time, the market for the artist would have been depressed and would have resulted in a *fair market value* much lower than that set by the donor's appraisers.

If one looks for a close parallel in the fine art market, the closest would probably be the sale of signed prints. The technology is available to produce any number of prints, but artists and dealers know that the art market has finite limits and it will be difficult if not impossible to sustain the asking the price. The number on offer of any one subject is, therefore, deliberately controlled to the amount the market can absorb—the usual limit is around 1,000 copies—as is the total number by one artist (many subjects) on offer at any one time.

A more immediate parallel can be found in the limited edition copies of cel set-ups that are common in the animation art market today. These are very popular subjects, with extremely high public recognition factors, and they are very carefully selected for their desirability to collectors. They are usually numbered, signed by the animator, and accompanied by a certificate of authenticity. The number in each issue varies, with the bulk of them under 1,000 copies and a few as high as 5,000. They very rarely exceed that number. In general, the lower the number issued, the higher the asking price.

There are two key issues in methodology that relate specifically to the appraisal of animated art collections. The first is the issue of price. In the absence of hard figures from actual sales of artwork from the collection being appraised, it is not sufficient to quote prices for animated art drawn from the world of animation and from any era in the history of animation. Comparable values can only be deduced from the sale of comparable art, and in the absence of such data, the appraiser should adopt a very conservative position on pricing. Unit pricing is particularly sensitive when dealing with thousands of units.

The second issue is volume. It is the nature of animation production that a very large number of works of art, cels, backgrounds and drawings are produced for every minute of moving image that appears on the screen. There is a temptation to assume that because one cel set-up is marketable any number of cel set-ups from the same production will be marketable. There is a law of diminishing returns in the art world and if the market is saturated, or near the saturation point, the price will start to decline. It is difficult to predict in advance where that point will be, but it is probably well short of 20,000 cels!

There is also the question of quality. Appraisers cannot assume that all cels are equal. It is the nature of animation production that a great many cels do not feature the lead characters in poses that art buyers would find desirable, or do not feature lead characters at all. Many of the cels are fragments that cannot be combined into a complete character, and if marketable at all would be marketable at very reduced prices. The *reasoned justifications* or *informed opinions,* which is all we can expect from appraisers, may differ, but the methodology, consistently applied, should avoid situations where one appraiser estimates that 25 percent of a collection of animated art is marketable, another estimates 10 percent, and a third estimates 2 percent!

For a precise assessment of the marketability of the cels in a collection each cel should be examined individually. Because of the vast quantity of artwork associated with animation collections, appraisers may resort to *sampling.* Sampling is a dubious approach to estimating the number of marketable units in an animation collection unless it is carried out with as close an approximation to science that statistics will allow. To be statistically valid the samples have to be *random,* based on a mathematically structured selection from the entire number of production files, *representative,* so that the different groupings, or in this case productions, are equally surveyed and *large,* or large enough to compensate for statistical errors.

The whole concept of sampling in appraising works of art can be questioned. Would an art gallery faced with the acquisition of a large collection of drawings use sampling to establish quality and price? Surely the only way to determine the absolute number of cel set-ups (or individual cels and drawings) and their *fair market value* is to count them, examine them, and assess them one by one. That this will add to the cost of the appraisal is undeniable. The irony is that it is precisely because the collection is so large that an accurate count, and not one based on sampling, is essential. Multipliers tend to distort the appraisals of all moving image collections, and when dealing with 250,000 items in an animation collection even very small variations in the multipliers can result in very significant differences in the valuations.

The sales comparison approach should be based on a one-on-one comparison, with the animated art valued individually. In evaluating collections en masse, the assumption appears to be that, with rare exceptions, all animation art is equal, regardless of content. Market prices, however, are closely allied to content, with wide differences in prices between productions and between cel set-ups from the same production.

Here, too, a rigorous *archival* appraisal should precede any attempt at a *monetary* appraisal. It should be clear that in the case of an animation studio donating all its production files (scripts, storyboards, preliminary and final art work, voice and music, and sound-effects tracks, etc.), it is the completeness of the collection documenting every aspect of production that makes it invaluable for research and education. It is, however, very difficult to place a value on this, and it should *not* be based on a percentage of the value assigned to the cel set-ups as derived from market comparisons. This value should be assessed before calculating the fair market value of the cel set-ups.

Related Documentation

It is part of the responsibility of the custodial archivist to acquire as much documentation as possible related to the film and video acquisitions. They should help establish the *provenance,* and allow researchers to study the context in which the works were created. Such documentation could include: scripts (drafts, shooting scripts and final cutting copies—copies of the script that conform to the film as edited); stills (shots from the film or video, on the set photos, and publicity shots); set designs; costume designs; production files (correspondence, contracts, schedules, etc.); and reviews. In the case of films that are computer generated, or that contain computer-generated sequences such as special effects, this should include the software that would enable an archivist or a researcher to play back the digital signal for review or duplication.

Appraising the *fair market value* of the stills and scripts is relatively uncomplicated using the *market comparison* approach. There is an established market for stills centered on stores specializing in moving image literature and memorabilia, although there are still copyright issues that have not yet been resolved. Scripts are also sold in such stores and like stills are regularly offered at auction in sales and via the Internet. The price of stills will vary widely with age, rarity, and demand (the issue of cult personalities, either short-term such as the star of the latest blockbuster, or long term such as the James Dean phenomenon), and in the case of scripts whether they are marked-up copies associated with a well-known director or star.

Placing a value on set and costume designs and production files is more difficult. It will vary with the perceived importance of the film or video, the completeness of the record, and its *research value*. This is a term that is difficult to define as it implies an ability to predict what archival resources will be in demand at some time in the future, and all our experience to date illustrates that we are unable to do that with any confidence. Valuations will inevitably be more subjective, although experienced appraisers will be able to draw on precedents to develop comparative values.

Physical Factors

There are a number of physical factors that may have an impact on valuation:

Is the physical condition of the material being donated such that the recipient institution will be forced to take urgent conservation measures before the material can be accessible to researchers and the public? The Transamerica case referred to earlier was one in which the court decided that the cost of preserving the collection should be deducted from the valuation proposed by the donors. In that case, however, the court did allow the full replacement cost for the large library of 16mm prints that were also donated, and contemporary market values for related documentation such as scripts, stills, and pressbooks.

Other examples are original negatives or single prints that must be protected with reference copies before there can be any public access; deteriorating film stock that must be isolated and copied; magnetic recordings or films on obsolete formats that must be copied before they can be viewed; animation cel drawings that need to be separated and stored in acid-free folders. These are all costs that may affect the valuation.

In determining replacement value has the redundancy factor in many moving image collections been considered? Examples are multiple prints or reference copies that are well beyond the requirements of the recipient institution for both long-term preservation and public access; production elements in sound and image that are technically substandard or slight variations from the shots selected with no aesthetic or commercial value, and sequences that were edited out of the version released to the public with the approval of the creative team responsible for the production.

In determining replacement value, has the format in which the recipient institution would choose to hold the work been considered? Would the institution actually purchase a 70mm or 65mm print of a film that was also released in 35mm? Would the institution actually purchase an analog magnetic recording if a digital format were available?

In 1998 a major Canadian university received a deposit of a very large quantity of production elements representing sixteen feature film projects. It was the second deposit from the production company—the first, consisting of the elements for thirty-four projects, had been valued at $2 million Canadian—and the stated intention of the principles in the company was to establish an archive of all their work at the university. In both the first and second deposits there were no transfer of rights beyond the right of the university to use the works for educational purposes on campus. There was no descriptive inventory or even a complete listing of the elements. In all cases the masters for each title were still held by the laboratories to manufacture further distribution copies. It was agreed that these would be deposited in due course, but in the absence of an inventory it was unclear what the masters for each title were or where they were held.

In reviewing the methodology to be applied in appraising the value of the second deposit, it was agreed that the disposition of the master material, primarily analog or digital videotape, had to be clarified *before* the material on deposit could be satisfactorily appraised, from either an archival or a monetary perspective. For example, if the production elements now on deposit are the sole surviving elements, and the title is appraised as having *archival* value, they will have far greater *monetary* value than if the master material is safely held in a laboratory, or in another repository. Conversely, if the masters, and protective masters, are in good condition, and will be deposited in accordance with a schedule to be negotiated by the university and the producers, a number of the production elements may not meet the university's selection criteria.

There is one important aspect of moving images that must be considered, particularly from the perspective of a university. Regardless of their *informational* value, moving images also have a *cultural* value that is difficult to define. They document the society in which they are produced, reflecting change and influencing change in equal measure. They also play a very important role in documenting and diffusing the other arts, and in making them accessible in the country of production and across the world.

Moving images have physical characteristics that further complicate appraisal and compound both the cost and the complexity of selection and processing. For example, the concept of the original versus copies, which can have a significant impact on the valuation of manuscript records, does not always apply in the case of film or videotape productions of the past fifty years, and will probably not apply at all in the case of digital recordings. Ideally the archives will acquire the original cut camera negative in the case of a film production (the negative that conforms to the edited work print) and an interpositive copy (fine grain) from which a duplicate negative can be struck. Prints and other reference copies can then be struck from the duplicate negative. This applies to the visual elements for almost all films in the pre-digital era. The master sound track (final mix) for films produced in the past forty years, however, will normally be a magnetic recording. This is a composite track made up of dialog tracks, music tracks, effects tracks, natural sound tracks, etc. The original elements are only valuable if there is a need to reconstitute the master track, or the sound elements could be marketed as stock sound (as visual elements are sold as stock shots). This is not an activity in which archives normally engage, and in fact it is a highly specialized activity carried out by very few stock shot libraries. The same is true of the visual elements that were not used in the final editing of the production. These are normally categorized as *trims* (the footage that is cut from individual shots) or *overs* (the *out-takes,* or footage that was not selected for inclusion in final editing). There may, however, be footage and sound that is archivally valuable in the *overs*, especially if they consist of interviews conducted for documentary productions and the interviews are technically acceptable and reasonably complete. *Overs* that are shots or sequences (shots that have been edited) should be appraised as item acquisitions. Where they are unique and irreplaceable, because either the subject is dead or the scene is no longer accessible, they may be valuable enough as accessions in their own right.

If *all* the material shot and recorded for a moving image production is available and on deposit, the question then is what needs to be preserved in order to adequately protect the production in the long term? The answer depends to some extent on the nature of the technology employed in arriving at the copy that is eventually distributed to the public.

In the case of a film production, acquisition of the original negative and an interpositive should be sufficient to protect the picture, although it would be prudent to acquire a duplicate negative as well, as this is the element that goes to the laboratory to strike new prints. Acquisition of the master magnetic track, the final mix, will protect the sound and allow the archives to strike reference copies as either film or video copies.

Video productions may originate from film elements or tape elements for picture, but almost always have magnetic components for sound. The film elements will be transferred to videotape for editing purposes and the final edited version will remain on videotape. The film elements are the originals but they are not required to protect the master videotape. It can be argued that in the case of a catastrophe there may be a need to reconstitute the master videotape, but it will be infinitely cheaper to strike a preservation videotape copy in the format adopted for the master and store that in a separate location.

The same principles apply to videotape *trims* and *overs*. Unless the unused shots and/or sequences have archival value in their own right, there is no need to retain them in order to protect the title.

There are no easy answers to the monetary appraisal of moving images. The methodology that has evolved is, in many cases, difficult to defend against either the charge that the assessment is subjective, particularly when cultural and historic values are involved, or that the assessment is formulaic on cost replacement or comparative market values, without sufficient consideration of the content and the nature of the material being assessed. This is no reason to avoid the process. Offering donors the monetary appraisal of their gift for tax advantages is now one of the most powerful tools that archivists have to persuade them to part with their possessions. It is, however, a tool that must be used responsibly or governments may act to limit its usefulness or remove it entirely.

Notes

1. Aaron Milrad, *Artful Ownership: Art Law, Valuation and* Commerce *in the United States, Canada and Mexico* (Washington, D.C.: American Society of Appraisers, 2000) 219.

2. Richard Lochead, Paper presented to the Association of Moving Image Archivists Conference, Montreal, November 1999.

3. Milrad, *Artful Ownership*, 52.

4. C.T.C. 636 at p.644, the Estate of A. M. Collings Henderson, *Bank of New York v. Minister of National Revenue* (1973). Affirmed in two Court Of Appeal Hearings in 1975.

5. Many of the facts that follow are taken from a summary of the arbitration panel decision released on 3 August, 1999, entitled *In the Matter of the Zapruder Film,* as attached to a U.S. Department of Justice press release of that date.

6. *Zapruder Film,* 3.

7. *Zapruder Film,* 4.

8. *Zapruder Film,* 8.

9. Milrad, *Artful* Ownership, 120.

10. *Zapruder Film,* 8.

11. Canadian Cultural Property Export Review Board, *Review Board Policies and Guidelines for Applications for Certification of Archival Audiovisual and Related Material.* Ottawa: Canadian Cultural Property Export Review Board, 2000.

12. Johnson, Steve, *Appraising Audiovisual Media: A Guide for Attorneys, Trust Officers, Insurance Professionals, and Archivists in Appraising Films, Videos, Photographs, Recordings, and other Audiovisual Assets* (Washington, D.C.: Association for Educational Communications and Technology, 1993).

13. Appraisal Standard Board of the Appraisal Foundation, *Uniform Standards of Professional Appraisal Practice.* (Washington, D.C.: The Appraisal Foundation, 1999) Foreword.

14. Canadian tax law made this practice very advantageous because the capital gain, the difference between the value at which the works were purchased and the value they were appraised at as gifts, was also exempt from taxation as a gift to a designated institution.

Conclusion

Hugh Taylor, Canada's great gift to archive lore and learning, summed up much of the discourse on archival theory by insisting that all archival activity should be seen as "an intellectual discipline based on the philosophical study of ideas, not an empirical discipline based on the scientific study of fact." There is obviously "more to the appraising of records than appraising records," as the literature on appraisal theory will attest, but there does not yet appear to be a sound set of ideas on appraisal that will breed consensus.

Appraisal is much more than methodology, which is a way of applying policies and standards, and more than strategy, but it is becoming evident that it is easier to say what appraisal *is not* than to define what it *is*.

There are no scientific "facts" on appraisal in this study, and precious little in the way of philosophy. What I have tried to do is to set out a few guidelines that may prove useful in assessing moving images.

What should be clear is that analysis of the facts surrounding a single work, a collection, or a whole archive of moving images is an essential prerequisite to the appraisal process. You should not appraise what you do not know and you must know the work in context, in relation to other works and to the creators and the administrative unit that sponsored the work, and to the particular economic and social conditions and the ideological framework in which it was created and distributed. Context and subtext. Only then will you know whether the work has archival value *for your archive* (it may have little or no value to another archive) or even it falls within your collecting mandate.

Even if you know everything there is to know about the work, you then have to move into the realm of speculation about its continuing value, and if it is your responsibility to assess its monetary value as well, there will be even more prediction involved. Nils Bohr's wry observation that "prediction is always difficult, especially about the future," is a reality with which all archivists have to contend.

No single descriptor of a potential acquisition should be a determining factor if it stands alone. Old age must be respected, but if the work is the third or fourth copy, and an inferior one as well, old age may not be enough. The relationship to other works, or to other documents in the collection may be enough, but if it adds nothing to our knowledge or our understanding it should not be a deciding factor. The work may be unique but so banal in subject matter and so poor in execution that it has no discernable value, except perhaps to the person who created it. There are no convincing formulas that apply, and it is usually a combination of factors that tip the scales in favor of retention or rejection.

To the vast bulk of works that lie between those that obviously have value and those that have no apparent value (at least to the appraiser striving to remain objective—all moving images have some value to someone) the archivist must bring knowledge, experience, and an open mind willing to learn more about other people's lives, and other worlds outside his own. Moving images operate on many levels and the appraiser must search for value in what is shown and what is absent. One of the hallmarks in gender studies, for example, is the absence of women, as well as their role. The same is true of persons of color. Whether purportedly fiction or nonfiction, the moving images have both surface realities and contextual realities, a relationship between the image-maker and the work and the audience and the work that may be more important than the images themselves.

Archivists sometimes refer to the "image of society" that results from the interaction of citizens and their government that is revealed in the records of transactions. It is the responsibility of the archivist to capture and convey that image to future generations. Moving image archivists work with more concrete images, but they can just as easily distort the record with poor choices as do their colleages working with the written word. If the archives assumes a passive attitude to appraisal, "what will come will be appraised," somewhat akin to Jenkinson's original position on public records, the "image of society" they will preserve will inevitably be skewed by the preponderance of "official" images from big government and big business. What will be missing is what Patricia Zimmerman calls "microhistories," the stories told by those using moving images at the margins of society and outside the industrial/capitalist mainstream.

The challenge of monetary appraisal simply complicates life for moving image archivists. Although the legal requirement is that they maintain an arm's length relationship to the actual appraisals submitted for either purchase or in association with gifts for tax benefits, they cannot escape the constant donor question, "What is it worth?" The recent spate of publicity on valuations that soar into the stratosphere, with the Zapruder film leading the pack, has only made donors more sensitive to the dollar value of their gifts.

In many tax jurisdictions archivists are expected to value donations under certain dollar limits, so that they must be conversant with the process, and in any case they must know the qualities of a good appraisal and the qualifications of a good appraiser so that they can advise their donors.

Monetary appraisal is as contentious and as frustrating as archival appraisal, marked by the same absence of standards and approved practices. The methodologies that have been developed are all suspect on assessments of intrinsic value, or in reliability in the search for comparable values. In a far from perfect world, monetary appraisal remains a necessary evil, like appraisal itself. With all its flaws, however, it remains a vital stimulus for the transfer of private property of cultural significance to public institutions.

Archivists will be debating appraisal theory and practice for years to come in the hope of raising appraisal out of that gray area between science and art. It has been described as a craft, but it is more than that: it is bound up with the key ideas in the philosophy of archives and the historic role of the archivist as the custodian of memory. In an age of abundance, in the volume of records if not in the budgets of archives, and in the coming age of digital conversion and media integration, the theory and practice of appraisal will continue to be the archivist's greatest challenge.

Bibliography

Agnew, Ella. "Making Photographic Sense: Appraisals of Photography and Film Collections." In *Legal Affairs and Management Symposium, 28 February-1March 1993*. Ottawa: Canadian Museums Association, 1993.

Alexander, Philip N. and Helen W. Samuels. "The Roots of 128: A Hypothetical Documentation Strategy." *American Archivist* 50 (fall 1987): 518-31.

Allerstrand, Sven. "The Preservation of Television Programmes in a National Archive: the Swedish Experience." In *Panorama of Audiovisual Archives*. London: BBC Data, 1986.

Alves-Netto, Cosme, Paulina Fernandez-Jurado, Hector Garcia-Mesa, and Manuel Gonzales-Casanova. "Latin America." In *Problems of Selection in Film Archives*. Brussels: International Federation of Film Archives, 1982.

Amtmann, Bernard. *Appraisals, Appraisers and 'Fair Market Value.'* Montreal: Montreal Book Auctions, Catalogue 109, 1978.

Appraisal Foundation, Appraisal Standard Board. *Uniform Standards of Professional Appraisal Practice*. Washington, D.C.: Appraisal Foundation, 1999.

Arbaugh, Dorothy. "Motion Pictures and the Future Historian." *American Archivist* 2 (1939): 106-14.

Arlen, Michael J. *Living-Room War*. New York: Viking Press, 1969.

————. *The Camera Age*. New York: Farrar Straus Giroux, 1981.

Arnheim, Rudolf. *Film as Art*. London: Cambridge University Press, 1957.

Atherton, Jay. "From Life Cycle to Continuum: Some Thoughts on the Records Management-Archives Relationship." *Archivaria* 21 (winter 1985-1986): 43-51.

Australia. National Film and Sound Archive. "Selection/Acquisition Policy and Guidelines for Film, Television and Documentation:

Policy Document, August, 1990." *Phonographic Bulletin* 58 (1991): 32-53.

Babcock, Henry A. *Appraisal Principles and Procedures.* Washington, D.C.: American Society of Appraisers, 1989.

Bachmann, Gideon. "Reappraisals: A Novel Look at Some Uses of the Cinematic Past." *Film Quarterly* 26 (1972/75): 10-14.

Bailey, Catherine. "From the Top Down: The Practice of Macro-Appraisal." *Archivaria* 43 (spring 1997) 89-128.

Baldizzone, Jose and Pierre Guibbert, eds. "Cinema et histoire, histoire du cinema." *Cahiers de la cinémathèque* 35/36, 1982.

Barkhausen, Hans. "Probleme der Filmarchivierung." *Archivar* 20 (1964): 361-68.

Barnouw, Erik. *Documentary: A History of the Non-Fiction Film.* New York: Oxford University Press, 1974.

_____. *The Sponsor: Notes on a Modern Potentate.* New York: Oxford University Press, 1978.

Baudot, Marcel. "Les triages et élimination." In *Manuel d'Achivistique: Théorie et Pratique des Archives Publiques.*" Paris: SEVPEN, 1970.

Bauer, G. Philip. *The Appraisal of Current and Recent Records.* (National Archives Staff Information Circular, no. 13) Washington, D.C.: National Archives and Records Service, 1946.

Baumhoher, Hermine M. "Motion Pictures become Federal Records." *American Archivist* 15 (1952): 15-26.

_____. "Film Records Management." *American Archivist* 19 (1956), 248-55.

Bautier, Robert-Henri. "Triages et éliminations des documents d' archives." *Archives, Bibliothèques, Collections Documentation* 9, (1955): 247-51.

Bearman, David A. and Richard H. Lytle. "The Power of Provenance." *Archivaria* 21 (1985-86): 14-27.

Beaumont, Roger A. "Images of War: Films as Documentary History." *Military Affairs* 55 (1971): 5-7.

Bellardo, Lewis J. and Lynn Lady Bellardo. *A Glossary for Archivists, Manuscript Curators and Records Managers.* Chicago: Society of American Archivists, 1992.

Benbert, T. Michael. "A Relationship of Constrained Anxiety: Historians and Film," *History Teacher.* 6 (1973) 555-68.

Bergeron, Rosemary. "The Selection of Televison Productions for Archival Preservation." *Janus* 1 (1991): 74-86.

Bergman, Andrew. *We're in the Money*. New York: Viking, 1971.

Berkeley, Edmund Jr. "The Archives and Appraisals." *Georgia Archive* 5, (1977) 51-63.

Birrell, Andrew. "The Tyranny of Tradition." *Archivaria* 10 (summer, 1980): 249-52.

Bluern, A. William. *Documentary in American Television: Form, Function, Methods*. New York: Hastings House, 1965.

Blumler, Jay G. and Denis McQuail. *Television in Politics*. Chicago: University of Chicago, 1969.

Boles, Frank and Julia Marks Young. *Archival Appraisal*. New York: Neal-Schuman, 1991.

Boles, Frank and Mark Greene. "'Et tu, Schellenberg'? Thoughts on the Dagger of American Appraisal Theory." *American Archivist* 56 (summer 1996): 298-310.

Bonneau, Germain. "Balises pur l'évaluation et le traitment des chutes de films: réflexion." *Archives* 25 (1993): 3-15.

Booms, Hans. "Society and the Formation of a Documentary Heritage: Issues in the Appraisal of Archival Sources." *Archivaria* 24 (summer 1987): 69-107.

Borde, Raymond, ed. "La Cinémathèque Française: recherche de la vérité." *Cahiers de la Cinémathèque* 22, (1977).

———. "Pas de sélection!" In *Problems of Selection in Film Archives*. Brussels: International Federation of Film Archives, 1982.

———. *Les Cinémathèques*. Paris: L'Age d'Homme, 1983.

Bowser, Eileen. "The Brighton Project: An Introduction." *Quarterly Review of Film Studies* 4, (1979): 507-50.

Bradley, John G. "Motion Pictures as Government Archives." *Society of Motion Picture Engineers Journal* 25, (1956): 653-60.

———. "A National Film Library—The Problem of Selection." *Society of Motion Picture Engineers Journal* 47 (1946): 65-72.

Brichford, Maynard J. *Scientific and Technological Documentation: Archival Evaluation and Processing of University Records Relating to Technology*. Urbana: University of Illinois, 1969.

———. *Archives and Manuscripts: Appraisal and Accessioning* Chicago: Society of American Archivists, 1977.

Briggs, Asa. "Problems and Possibilities in the Writing of Broadcasting History." *Media Culture and Society* 2 (1978): 5-13.

Brooks, Philip C. "The Selection of Records for Preservation." *American Archivist* 3 (1940): 221-34.

————. "Archival Procedures for Planned Records Retirement." *American Archivist* 11 (October 1948):308-15.

————. *What Records Shall We Preserve?* (Staff Information Papers, no. 19) Washington, D.C.: National Archives and Records Service, 1971.

Brothman, Brian. "Orders of Value: Probing the Theoretical Terms of Archival Practice." *Archivaria* 32 (summer 1991): 78-100.

Brown, Thomas E. "The Evolution of an Appraisal Theory for Automated Records." *Archives and Museum Informatics* 1 (fall 1987): 49-51.

Brownlow, Kevin. *The War, The West, and The Wilderness.* London: Secker & Warburg, 1979.

Bruckhardt, F. "Les éliminations." *Gazette des Archives* 108, (1980): 155-58.

Bryant, Steve. *The Television Heritage: Television Archiving Now and in an Uncertain Future.* London: British Film Institute, 1989.

————. "FIAT Guidelines for Selection and Preservation of Television Programme Material—A National Perspective." In *FIAT Minutes and Working Papers, Vith Seminar, 5-9 September 1993, Sofia, Bulgaria.*

Burke, Frank G. "The Future Course of Archival Theory in the United States." *American Archivist* 44 (1981): 40-46.

Butler, Ivan. *"To Encourage the Art of the Film": The Story of the British Film Institute.* London: Robert Hale, 1971.

Calas, Marie-France. "Legal Deposit of Audiovisual Materials in National Collections." *Phonographic Bulletin* 56 (1990): 2-9.

Cameron, Alan. "Should the Creator of Records Consider the Needs of Future Research." *Janus* 2 (1992): 75-79.

Canada. National Archives of Canada. *Documents that Move and Speak: Audiovisual Archives in the New Information Age.* Munich: Saur, 1992.

Canada. Canadian Cultural Property Export Review Board. *Review Board Policies and Guidelines for Applications for Certification of Archival Audiovisual and Related Material.* Ottawa: Canadian Cultural Property Export Review Board, 2000.

Canada. Task Force on the Preservation and Enhanced Use of Canada's Audio-Visual Heritage. *Fading Away: Strategic Options to Ensure the Protection of and Access to Our Audio-Visual Memory.* Ottawa: National Archives of Canada, 1995.

Cappon, Lester J. "What, Then, is There to Theorize About?" *American Archivist* 45 (1982)19-25.

Carnes, Mark C. ed. *Past Imperfect: History According to the Movies.* New York: Henry Holt, 1995.

Carroll, Carman. *Report to the Canadian Cultural Property Export Review Board Concerning the Certification of Archival Film, Music and Related Collections.* Ottawa: Canadian Cultural Property Export Review Board, 1997.

Caya, Marcel. "L'évaluation monétaire: une instrument d'acquisition." *Archives* 28, (1996-97): 49-58.

Cherchi Usai, Paolo. *The Death of Cinema: History, Cultural Memory and the Digital Dark Age.* London: British Film Institute, 2001.

Collet, Jean. "Research and Creation at the Institut National de l'Audiovisuel." *European Broadcasting Union Review* 32, (1981): 17-21.

Collingridge, John H. "The Selection of Archives for Permanent Preservation." *Archivum* 6 (1956): 25-35.

Connors, Thomas. "Appraising Public Television Programs: Toward an Interpretive and Comparative Evaluation Model." *American Archivist* 63 spring/summer 2000): 152-74.

Cook, Michael. *Archives Administration: A Manual for Intermediate and Smaller Organizations.* Folkestone, England: William Dawson, 1977.

———. "Appraisal Criteria: Research Values." In *Records Appraisal: Proceedings of a Society of Archivists In-Service Training Course, 21-23 September 1983.* Chicago: Society of Archivists, 1985.

Cook, Terry. "The Tyranny of the Medium: A Comment on Total Archives." *Archivaria* 9 (1979-80): 141-49.

———. "Media Myopia." *Archivaria* 12 (1981): 146-157.

———. "Documentation Strategy." *Archivaria* 34 (summer 1992): 181-91.

———. "Mind Over Matter: Towards a New Theory of Archival Appraisal." In *The Archival Imagination: Essays in Honour of Hugh A. Taylor,* ed. Barbara L. Craig. Ottawa: Association of Canadian Archivists, 1992.

———. "Another Brick in the Wall: Terry Eastwood's Masonry and Archival Walls, History, and Archival Appraisal." *Archivaria* 37 (spring 1994): 96-103.

————. "What is Past is Prologue: A History of Archival Ideas Since 1898, and the Future Paradigm Shift." *Archivaria* 43 (spring 1997): 17-63.

————. *The Archival Appraisal of Records Containing Personal Information: A RAMP Study with Guidelines.* Paris: UNESCO, 1991.

Coughie, John, ed. *Television: Ideology and Exchange.* (BFI Television Monograph, no. 9) London: British Film Institute. 1978.

Coultass, Clive. "Film Preservation: The Archives." In *The Historian and Film,* ed. Paul Smith. Cambridge: Cambridge University, 1976.

————. "Film as an Historical Source: Its Use and Abuse." *Archives* 8 (1977): 12-19.

————. "The Selection of Non-fiction Film." In *Problems of Selection in Film Archives.* Brussels: International Federation of Film Archives, 1982.

Cox, Richard J. and Helen W. Samuels. "The Archivists' First Responsibility: A Research Agenda to Improve the Identification and Retention of Records of Enduring Value." *American Archivist* 51 (winter-spring 1988): 28-42.

Craig, Barbara, ed. "The Acts of the Appraisers: the Context, the Plan and the Record." *Archivaria* 34 (1992).

Cugier, Alphonse, ed. "Cinema et histoire, histoire du cinema." *Cahiers de la Cinémathèque* 10/11 (1975).

Cummings, Bruce. *War and Television.* London: Verso, 1992.

Darter, Lewis, J. "Records Appraisal: A Demanding Task." *Indian Archives* 19 (1969) 1-9.

Davidson, Steve and Gregory Lukow, eds. *The Administration of Televison Newsfilm and Videotape Collections: A Curatorial Manual.* Miami: Wolfson Center, 1995.

Deming, Barbara. "The Library of Congress Film Project: Exposition of a Method." *Library of Congress Quarterly Journal* 2 (1944) 3-36.

————. *Running Away From Myself: A Dream Portrait of America Drawn From the Films of the 40s.* New York: Grossman, 1969.

Dick, Ernest J. "Through the Rearview Mirror: Moving Image and Sound Archives in 1990s." *Archivaria* 28 (1989): 68-73.

————. "An Archival Acquisition Strategy for the Broadcast Records of the Canadian Broadcasting Corporation." *Historical Journal of Film. Radio and Television* 11 (1991): 253-68.

————. "Corporate Memory in Sound and Visual Records." In *The Records of American Business,* ed. James M. O'Toole. Chicago: Society of American Archivists, 1997.

Dick, Ernest J. et al. "Total Archives Come Apart." *Archivaria* 11 (winter 1980-81): 224-27.

Duranti, Luciana. "Diplomatics." *Archivaria* 28 (summer 1989): 7-27; 29 (winter 1989-90): 4-17; 30 (summer 1990): 4-20; 31 (winter 1990-91): 10-25; 32 (summer 1991): 6-24; 33 (winter 1991-92): 6-24.

————. "So? What Else Is New? the Ideology of Appraisal Yesterday and Today." In *Archival Appraisal: Theory and Practice,* ed. Christopher Hives. Vancouver: Archives Association of British Columbia, 1990.

————. "The Concept of Appraisal and Archival Theory." *American Archivist* 57 (spring 1994): 328-45.

Ducharme, Daniel and Carol Couture. "L''évaluation en archivistique, evolution et tendances: etude bibliographique 1980-1995. *Archives* 28 (1996-1997): 59-98.

Duchein, Michel. "Les procedures de tri dans les archives départementales." *Gazette des Archives* 77 (1972) 75-77.

Eamon, Greg and Rosemary Bergeron. "Selection Factors in Audio-Visual Archives." Appendix B. *Fading Away: Strategic Options to Ensure the Protection of and Access to Our Audio-Visual Memory.* Ottawa: National Archives of Canada, 1995.

Eastwood, Terry. "Towards a Social Theory of Appraisal." In *The Archival Imagination: Essays in Honour of Hugh A. Taylor,* ed. Barbara L. Craig. Ottawa: Association of Canadian Archivists, 1992.

————. "How Goes It with Appraisal?" *Archivaria* 36 (autumn 1993): 111-21.

Eaton, Mick, ed. *Anthropology-Reality-Cinema: The Films of Jean Rouch.* London: British Film Institute, 1979.

Elton, Arthur. "The Film as Source Material for History." *ASLIB Proceedings* 7 (1955): 207-59.

European Association Inedits. *Jubilee Book: Essays on Amateur Film* Charleroi, Belgium: Association Européenne Inédits, 1997.

Evans, Frank B., comp. *The History of Archives Administration: A Select Bibliography.* Paris: UNESCO, 1979.

Evans, Frank B., Donald Harrison and Edwin A. Thompson, comps. "A Basic Glossary for Archivists, Manuscript Curators, and Records Managers." *American Archivist* 37 (1974): 415-35.

Evans, Gary. *John Grierson and the National Film Board: the Politics of Wartime Propaganda.* Toronto: University of Toronto, 1984.

Ferro, Marco. "Société du XXe siècle et histoire cinématographique." *Annales* 23 (1968): 581-85.

————. "Le film, une contre-analyse de la société?" *Annales.* 28 (1973): 109-24.

————. "The Fiction Film and Historical Analysis." In *The Historian and Film*, ed. Paul Smith. Cambridge: Cambridge University, 1976.

FIAF: See: International Federation of Film Archives.

FIAT: See: International Federation of Television Archives.

Fielding, Raymond. *The American Newsreel, 1911-1967.* Norman: University of Oklahoma, 1972.

————. *The March of Time, 1955-1972.* New York: Oxford University, 1978.

Fishbein, Meyer H. "Appraisal of Twentieth Century Records for Historical Use." *Illinois Libraries* 52 (1970): 154-62.

————. "A Viewpoint on Appraisal of National Records." *American Archivist* 53 (1970) 175-87.

Fledelius, Karsten, et al, eds. *History and the Audio-Visual Media: Studies in History, Film & Society.* Copenhagen: International Association for the Study of Media and History, vol. 1, 1979; vol. 2, 1980.

————. "Audiovisual History—the Development of a New Field of Research." *Historical Journal of Film, Radio and Television,* 9 (1989): 151-63.

Furhammar, Leif and Foike Isaksson. *Politics and Film.* New York: Praeger, 1971.

Grazzini, Giovanni. *La memoria negli occhi: Boleslaw Matuszewski, un pioniere del cinema.* Rome: Carocci, 1999.

Great Britain. Public Record Office. *Principles Governing the Elimination of Ephemeral or Unimportant Documents in Public or Pirvate Archives.* London: Public Record Office, n.d.

————. *New Perspectives on the Selection of Documents.* (R.A.D. Paper No. 4) London: Public Records Office, 1975.

Greene, Mark. "'The Surest Proof': A Utilitarian Approach to Appraisal." *Archivaria* 45 (spring 1998): 127-69.

Grenville, J. A. S. and Nicholas Pronay. "The Historian and Historical Films." *University Vision* 1 (1968): 3-5.

Grenville, J. A. S. *Film and History: the Nature of Film Evidence.*

Birmingham: University of Birmingham, 1971.

Guback, Thomas H. "Cultural Identity and Film in the European Economic Community." *Cinema Journal* 2 (1974): 2-17.

Haas, J. et al. *Appraising the Records of Modern Science and Technology: A Guide.* Boston: Massachusetts Institute of Technology, 1985.

Ham, F. Gerald. "The Archival Edge." *American Archivist* 58 (1975): 5-13.

———. "Archival Choices: Managing the Historical Record in an Age of Abundance." *American Archivist* 47 (winter 1984): 11-22.

———. *Selecting and Appraising Archives and Manuscripts.* Chicago: Society of American Archivists, 1993.

Hanford, Ann. *Recommended Standards and Procedures for Selection and Preservation of Television Programme Material: BBC Archival Policy and its Applications in FIAT.* Sofia, Bulgaria: International Federation of Television Archives, 1993.

Hanson, Stan. *The Monetary Appraisal of Archival Documents in Canada.* Ottawa: Association of Canadian Archivists, 1992.

Harrison, Helen P. *The Archival Appraisal of Sound Recordings and Related Materials: A RAMP Study with Guidelines.* Paris: UNESCO, 1987.

———. Ed. *Audiovisual Archives: A Practical Reader.* Paris: UNESCO, 1997.

Heckmann, Harald. "Television Archives in the Federal Republic of Germany." In *Panorama of Audiovisual Archives.* London: BBC Data, 1986.

Hedstrom, Margaret. "New Appraisal Techniques: the Effect of Theory on Practice." *Provenance* 7 (fall, 1989): 1-21.

Heesteren, Evelyn van. "The Use of Television Archives—Copyright and Related Rights." In *Panorama of Audiovisual Archives.* London: BBC Data, 1986.

Herrick, Doug. "Toward a National Film Collection: Motion Pictures at the Library of Congress." *Film Library Quarterly* 15 (1980) 5-25.

Hives, Christopher, ed. *Archival Appraisal: Theory and Practice.* Vancouver: Archives Association of British Columbia, 1990.

Houston, Penelope. "The Nature of the Evidence." *Sight and Sound* 56 (1967): 88-92.

———. *Keepers of the Frame: the Film Archives.* London: British Film Institute, 1994.

Hughes, William. "The Evaluation of Film as Evidence." In *The Historian and Film*, ed. Paul Smith. Cambridge: Cambridge University, 1976.

Hull, David Steward. *Film in the Third Reich: A Study of the German Cinema, 1953-1945.* Berkeley: University of California, 1969.

Hull, Felix. *The Use of Sampling Techniques in the Retention of Records: A RAMP Study with Guidelines.* Paris: UNESCO, 1981.

———. "The Appraisal of Documents: Problems and Pitfalls." *Journal of the Society of Archivists* 6 (April 1980): 287-91.

International Federation of Film Archives. *A Handbook for Film Archives.* Brussels: International Federation of Film Archives, 1980.

———. *Problems of Selection in Film Archives.* Brussels: International Federation of Film Archives, 1980.

International Federation of Television Archives. *Recommended Standards and Procedures for Selection and Preservation of Television Programme Material.* Paris: International Federation of Television Archives, 1996.

———. *Panorama of Audiovisual Archives*, ed. Dominique Saintville. London: BBC Data, 1986.

Jeavons, Clyde. "Selection in the National Film Archive of Great Britain." In *Problems of Selection in Film Archives.* Brussels: International Federation of Film Archives, 1980.

Jenkinson, Hilary. *A Manual of Archives Administration.* Oxford: Clarendon Press, 1922.

———. "Speech to the International Council on Archives." *Archivum* 1 (1951): 47-50.

———. "Modern Archives: Some Reflections on T. R. Schellenberg." *Journal of the Society of Archivists* 1 (april 1957): 148-49.

Johnson, Steve. *Appraising Audiovisual Media: A Guide for Attorneys, Trust Officers, Insurance Professionals, and Archivists in Appraising Films, Videos, Photographs, Recordings and Other Audiovisual Assets.* Washington, D.C.: Association for Educational Communication and Technology, 1993.

Kalenski, Gustav. "Record Selection." *American Archivist* 59 (1976): 25-45.

Karr, Larry, "The American Situation." In *Problems of Selection in Film Archives.* Brussels: International Federation of Film Archives, 1982.

Kahlenberg, Friedrich P. "Toward a Vital Film Culture: Film Archives in Germany." *Quarterly Review of Film Studies* 5 (1980): 255-61.

Klep, Paul M. M. "About Ethics of Appraisal of Archival Records."
    Janus 5 (1980): 253-61.
Klumpenhouwer, Richard. *Concepts of Value in the Archival Appraisal
    Literature: An Historical and Critical Analysis.* Master of Archival
    Studies Thesis, University of British Columbia, 1989.
Kofler, Birgit. *Legal Questions Facing Audiovisual Archives.* Paris:
    UNESCO, 1991.
Kohte, Wilhelm. "Uber Bild und Film Archive." *Der Archivar,* 13
    (1960): 2-14; 16 (1963): 189-98; 20 (1967): 361-68.
————. *Archives of Motion Pictures, Photographic Records and Sound
    Recordings: A Report Prepared for the XIIth International Con-
    gress on Archives, Moscow, August 21-25, 1972.* Paris: Interna-
    tional Council on Archives, 1972.
Kolsrud, Ole. "The Evolution of Basic Appraisal Principles." *American
    Archivist* 55 (winter 1992): 278-86.
Kracauer, Siegfried. *From Caligari to Hitler: A Psychological History
    of the German Film.* Princeton: Princeton University, 1947.
Kuehl, Jerry. "The Historian and Film." *Sight and Sound* 45 (1976):
    118-19.
Kuiper, John B. "The Historical Value of Motion Picture." *American
    Archivist* 51 (1968): 385-89.
Kula, Sam. *Bibliography of Film Librarianship.* London: The Library
    Association, 1967.
————. "Archiving Television: NFTSA and Broadcasts of National
    Historic Interest." *Association for Study of Canadian Radio and
    Television Bulletin* 17 (1982): 5-11.
————. "Audiovisual Documentation in Archives. *Southeast Asian
    Archives,* Special Issue (1983): 3-6.
————. "Film Archives at the Centenary of Film." *Archivaria* 40 (fall
    1995): 210-25.
————. "Some Observations on Audio-Visual Heritage Programs in
    Other Countries." Appendix D. *Fading Away: Strategic Options to
    Ensure the Protection of and Access to Our Audio-Visual Memory.*
    Ottawa: National Archives of Canada, 1995.
Laberge, Danielle. "Information, Knowledge, and Rights: the Preserva-
    tion of Archives as a Political and Social Issue." *Archivaria* 25
    (winter 1987-1988): 44-50.
Leab, Daniel J. "From 'Sambo' to 'Superspade': Some Problems in the
    Use of Film in Historical Research." *University Vision* 10
    (1973):41-8.

————. *From "Sambo" to "Superspade": The Black Experience in Motion Pictures.* Boston: Houghton Mifflin, 1975.

Leary, William H. *The Archival Appraisal of Photographs: A RAMP Study with Guidelines.* Paris: UNESCO, 1985.

Lindgren, Ernest. "The Selection of Films as Historical Records in the National Film Archives." *University Vision* 6 (1971): 15-25.

Lockwood, Elizabeth. "Imponderable Matters: the Influence of New Trends in History on Appraisal in the National Archives." *American Archivist* 53 (1990): 394-405.

Lovell, Alan and Jim Hilliel. *Studies in Documentary.* New York: Viking, 1972.

Low, Rachael. *Films of Comment and Persuasion of the 1950s.* London: George Allen & Unwin, 1979.

————. *Documentary and Educational Films of the 1930s.* London: George Allen & Unwin, 1979.

MacCann, Richard Dyer. *The People's Films: A Political History of U.S. Government Motion Pictures.* New York: Hastings House, 1973.

McCree, M. L. "Good Sense and Good Judgment: Defining Collections and Collecting." In *A Modern Archives Reader,* eds. Maygene F. Dabiels and Timothy Walch. Washington, D.C.: National Archives and Records Service, 1984.

McDonald, A. J. "Acquiring and Preserving Private Records: Cultural Versus Administrative Perspectives." *Archivaria* 38 (1994): 162-63.

McRanor, Shauna. "A Critical Analysis of Intrinsic Value." *American Archivist* 59 (fall 1996): 400-11.

Mamber, Stephen. *Cinema Verite in America: Studies in Uncontrolled Documentary.* Cambridge, Mass.: Massachusetts Institute of Technology, 1974.

Mander, Jerry. *Four Arguments for the Elimination of Television.* New York: Morrow Quill, 1978.

Mann, Sarah Ziebell. *American Moving Image Preservation, 1967-1987.* Master of Arts Thesis, University of Texas at Austin, 2000.

Matuszewski, Boleslaw. *Une Nouvelle Source de l'Histoire: Création d'un Dépot de Cinématographie Historique.* March, 1898.

————. *La Photographie Animée, Ce Qu'elle Est, Ce Qu'elle Doit Etre* August, 1898. Copies of both pamphlets are reproduced in *Boleslaw Matuszewski: Jego Pionierska Mysl Filmowa.* Warsaw: Filmoteca Polska. 1980.

Menne-Haritz, Angelika. "Appraisal or Documentation: Can We Appraise Archives By Selecting Content?" *American Archivist* 49 (1994): 528-42.

Miller Frederic. "Use, Appraisal and Research: A Case Study of Social History." *American Archivist* 49 (1986): 371-92.

Milrad, Aaron. *Artful Ownership: Art Law, Valuation and Commerce in the United Statesm Canada and Mexico.* Washington, D.C.: American Society of Appraisers, 2000.

Murphy, William. "Film at the National Archives: A Reference Article." *Film and History* 2 (1972): 7-13.

―――. "The Method of 'Why We Fight.'" *Journal of Popular Film* 1 (1972): 185-96.

Myrant, Glen and George P. Langlois, *Henri Langlois: First Citizen of Cinema.* New York: Twayne, 1995.

National Film Archives, British Film Institute. *Guide to the Selection of Films For Historical Preservation.* London: British Film Institute, 1959.

Nieuwenhof, Frans. "Feature Film as Reflection of Popular Mentality." *ICA Archival Review* 1 (1992): 34-43.

Norton, Margaret Cross. *Norton of Archives: the Writings of Margaret Cross Norton on Archival and Records Management,* ed. Thorton W. Mitchell. Carbondale: Southern Illinois University, 1975.

O'Connor, John E. and Martin A. Jackson, eds. *American History/American Film: Interpreting the Hollywood Image.* New York: Ungar, 1979.

Opela, Vladimir. "Problems of Selection of Film Materials and the Archival System in Czechoslovakia." In *Problems of Selection in Film Archives.* Brussels: International Federation of Film Archives, 1982.

―――. "What Future for Film Archiving in Eastern Europe? The Case of the Czech Republic." *FIAF Bulletin* 46 (April 1993): 3.

O'Toole. "On the Idea of Permanence." *American Archivist* 52 (winter 1989): 10-25.

Peace, Nancy E. "Deciding What to Save: Fifty Years of Theory and Practice." In *Archival Choices,* ed. Nancy E. Peace. Toronto: D.C. Heath, 1981.

Peterson, Ann. "Dr. Frankenstein Revisited: Creative Experiments in Archival Selection and Appraisal." *New Zealand Archivist* 4 (1982): 1-7.

Peterson, T. H. "The Gift and the Deed." In *A Modern Archives Reader*, eds. Maygene F. Daniels and Timothy Walch. Washington, D.C.: National Archives and Records Service, 1984.

Pinkett, Harold T. "Identification of Records of Continuing Value." *Indian Archives* 16 (1965): 54-61.

Postman, Neil. *Amusing Ourselves to Death: Public Discourse in the Age of Show Business*. New York: Penguin Books, 1985.

Powdermaker, Hortense. *Hollywood the Dream Factory: An Anthropologist Looks at the Movie-Makers*. Boston: Little, Brown, 1950.

Pronay, Nicholas. "The Newsreels: the Illusion of Actuality." In *The Historian and Film*, ed. Paul Smith. Cambridge: Cambridge University, 1976.

Pronay, Nicholas and D. W. Spring. *Propaganda, Politics and Film, 1918-1945*. London: Macmillan, 1982.

Rapport, Leonard. "No Grandfather Clause: Reappraising Accessioned Records." *American Archivist* 44 (1981): 143-50.

Raymond, Andrew and James O'Toole. "Up from the Basement: Archives, History and Public Administration." *Georgia Archive* 6 (fall 1978): 26-27.

Reed, Barbara. "Appraisal and Disposal." In *Keeping* Archives, ed. Judith Ellis. Port Melbourne, Australia: D. W. Thorpe, 1993.

Richards, Jeffrey. *Visions of Yesterday*. London: Routledge & Kegan Paul, 1975.

Rieger, Morris. "Modern Records Retirement and Appraisal Practice." *UNESCO Journal of Information Science, Librarianship and Archives Administration* 1 (1979): 200-209.

Rollins, Peter C. *Hollywood as Hisorian: American Film in a Cultural Context*. Lexington, Kentucky: University of Kentucky, 1983.

Rotha, Paul. *Documentary Film*. London, Faber, 1952.

Roud, Richard. *A Passion for Films: Henri Langlois and the Cinémathèque Française*. New York: Viking, 1983.

Ruhe, Karl. "Valuation for Federal Tax Purposes." *Antiquarian Bookman* 17 (1970): 558-41.

Saintville, Dominique, ed. "Les archives de la télévision: images de notre temps." *Problemes Audiovisuels*. 2 (1981) 1-52.

Samuels, Helen W. "Who Controls the Past?" *American Archivist* 49, (Spring 1986): 109-24.

———. "Improving Our Disposition: Documentation Strategy." *Archivaria* 33 (winter 1991-92): 125-40.

Samuels, Helen W. and Richard Cox. "The Documentation Strategy and Archival Appraisal Pronciples, A Different Perspective." *Archivaria* 38 (fall 1994): 11-36.

Sayre, Nora. *Running Time: Films of the Cold War.* New York: Doubleday, 1982.

Schellenberg, Theodore R. *Modern Archives: Principles and Techniques.* Chicago: University of Chicago, 1956.

———. *The Appraisal of Modern Public Records.* (Bulletin of the National Archives, no. 8) Washington, D.C.: National Archives and Records Service, 1956. Reprinted in *A Modern Archives Reader*, eds. Maygene F. Daniels and Timothy Walch. Washington, D.C.: National Archives and Records Service, 1984.

Shaheen, Jack, ed. *Nuclear War Films.* Carbondale, Ill.: Southern Illinois University Press, 1978.

Sink, Robert. "Appraisal: the Process of Choice." *American Archivist* 53 (summer 1990): 451-58.

Slide, Anthony. *Nitrate Won't Wait: Film Preservation in the United States.* Jefferson, North Carolina: McFarland, 1992.

Spehr, Paul. "United States Copyrihgt Law and the Library of Congress Collection of Television Broadcasts." In *Panorama of Audiovisual Archives.* London: BBC Data, 1986.

Smith, Anthony. *The Shadow in the Cave: the Broadcaster, the Audience and the State.* London: Quartet, 1976.

———. "Mixing Chemistry with Culture: Preserving Film and Television." *Royal Society of Arts Journal* (June 1981) 423-54.

Scientific Film Association. *The Evaluation of Scientific, Industrial and Medical Films.* London: Scientific Film Association. 1958.

Semenovicer, B. K. "State Registration and Archive Preservation of Audiovisual Materials in the USSR." *Sovetskoe Bibliotekovedeie* 2 (1973): 95-102.

Speed, Francis. "The Function of the Film as Historical Record." *African Notes* 6 (1968): 45-51.

Surowiec, Catherine A. *The Lumière Project: the European Archives a t the Crossroads.* Lisbon: ACCE, 1996.

Taylor, Hugh A. "Transformation in the Archives: Technological Adjustment or Paradigm Shift?" *Archivaria* 25 (winter 1987-1988): 12-28.

———. "The Totemic Universe: Appraising the Documentary Future." In *Archival Appraisal: Theory and Practice*, ed. Christopher Hive. Vancouver: Archives Associatoin of British Columbia, 1990.

————. "'The Conjuring Tent': News Documents as Valid Historical Evidence." In *Beyond the Printed Word: The Evolution of Canada's Broadcast News Heritage*, ed. Richard Lochead. Kingston: Quarry Press, 1991.

Turner, Allan B. "Issues in the Appraisal of Non-Traditional Records: Sound and Moving Images." In *Archival Appraisal: Theory and Practice*, ed. Christopher Hives. Vancouver: Archives Association of British Columbia, 1990.

Turner, Jane. *A Study of the Theory of Appraisal for Selection*. Master of Archival Studies Thesis, University of British Columbia, 1992.

UNESCO. *Final Report of the Expert Consultation on the Development of a Records and Archives Management Programme (RAMP) Within the Framework of the General Information Programme, 14-16 May, 1979*. Paris: UNESCO, 1979.

————. *Recommendation for the Safeguarding and Preservation of Moving Images. Adopted by the General Conference, Belgrade, 27 October, 1980*. Paris: UNESCO, 1981.

United States. Library of Congress. *Redefining Film Preservation, A National Plan: Recommendations of the Librarian of Congress in Consultation with the National Film Preservation Board*. Washington, D.C.: Library of Congress, 1994.

————. National Film Preservation Board. *Film Preservation 1993: A Study of the Current State of American Film Preservation*. Washington, D.C.: Library of Congress, 1993.

————. Librarian of Congress. *Television and Video Preservation 1997: A Report on the Current State of American Television and Video Preservation*. Washington, D.C.: Library of Congress, 1997.

————. Department of Justice. Press Release, 3 August, 1999. *In the Matter of the Zapruder Film*. Washington, D.C.: Department of Justice, 1999.

————. National Archives and Records Service, Committee on Intrinsic Value. *Intrinsic Value in Archival Materials*. (Staff Information Paper 21). Washington, D.C.: National Archives and Records Service, 1982.

Walden, David. "Stretching the Dollar: Monetary Appraisal of Manuscripts. *Archivaria* 2 (1980/81) 101-7.

Wallis, Howard L. "Motion Picture Incunabula in the Library of Congress." *Society of Motion Picture Engineers Journal* 42 (1944): 155-58.

Walters, Tyler O. "Contemporary Archival Appraisal methods and preservation decision-making." *American Archivist* 59 (1996): 322-38.

Wasson, Haidee. "The Cinematic Subtext of the Modern Museum: Alfred H. Barr and MoMA's Film Archive." *The Moving Image* 1 (spring 2001): 1-28.

Worth, Sol and John Adair. *Through Navajo Eyes: An Explora tion in Film, Communication and Anthropology.* Bloomington: Indiana University, 1975.

Zimmerman, Patricia. "Morphing History into Histories: From Amateur Film to the Archive of the Future." *The Moving Image* 1 (spring 2001): 109-30.

Zon Yahya, Habibah. "Preserving Television Transmissions: Strategies for Acquisition, Appraisal, Storage and Use." In *Proceedings of the 13th International Council on Archives, Beijing 2-7 September 1996.* Paris: International Council on Archives, 1996.

Index

About the author:

Sam Kula was born in Montreal, Canada, in 1932, and graduated with a degree in History from Concordia University in 1954. He trained as an archivist in the Manuscript Division of the National Archives of Canada for three years before leaving for London,where he acquired a Diploma in Librarianship from University College, University of London, and trained as a film archivist as Deputy Curator to Ernest Lindgren at the National Film and Television Archive of the British Film Institute. In 1962 he began a doctoral program in film and communications at the University of Southern California, where he worked and studied for the next five years. In 1968 he joined the newly established American Film Institute as its first archivist and assistant director. While at the AFI he initiated a national program in film preservation and established the American Film Institute Collection at the Library of Congress. In 1973 he returned to Canada to establish the National Film and Television Archives at the National Archives. During the past twenty-five years he has been active in developing archives and preservation programs throughout the world through executive positions in the International Federation of Film Archives and the International Federation of Television Archives and through seminars, workshops, and study missions carried out for UNESCO and the International Council on Archives. He wrote *The Archival Appraisal of Moving Images: A RAMP Study with Guidelines* for UNESCO, which was published in 1983. He has served on the executive of the Association of Moving Image Archivists for the past six years, as President for the past two years, and on the Board of AV Preservation Trust.CA since it was established in 1996. He is now an archival consultant and Special Advisor to the Canadian Cultural Property Export Review Board.